Dedicated to Lyle Mays and Naná Vasconcelos

A Sentry Guide to

**Popular, Jazz and Orchestral
Brazilian Music**

ISBN Paperback 978-1-989647-22-6

A Byrd Press Publication
Toronto
www.byrdpress.com
publisher@byrdpress.com

cover design R.H. Mason
interior art Felipe Silva

A Sentry Guide to

Popular, Jazz and Orchestral Brazilian Music

Table of Contents

Introduction

Nestled between the sun-kissed shores of the Atlantic and the lush expanse of the Amazon rainforest, Brazil pulsates with an energy that finds its purest expression in the rhythmic vibrancy of its music. From the bustling city streets of São Paulo to the vibrant cultural hubs of Salvador, the nation resonates with a symphony of sounds that mirrors the very essence of its people, their stories, and their collective dreams. Through the captivating melodies of its popular music, the improvisational spirit of its jazz, and the sweeping harmonies of its orchestral compositions, Brazil's musical legacy stands as a testament to the nation's enduring spirit, resilience, and unwavering passion for life.

This book is a comprehensive exploration of the diverse and dynamic world of Brazilian music, encompassing popular, jazz, and orchestral genres. It delves into the rich historical and cultural tapestry of Brazil, unveiling the profound significance of its music within the context of the nation's identity, heritage, and societal fabric. Through a meticulous examination of key musical movements, iconic figures, and seminal compositions, this book offers readers a profound understanding of the multifaceted nature of Brazilian music and its enduring impact on global cultural landscapes.

The initial chapters lay the groundwork by delving into the historical roots of Brazilian music, tracing its origins from the indigenous rhythms, colonial influences, and the infusion of African musical traditions. It unravels the unique fusion of these diverse cultural elements, shaping the distinct musical identity that defines Brazil's vibrant and varied music scene.

The book then delves deeply into the pulsating rhythms of samba, exploring its historical evolution, social significance, and its enduring role as a symbol of Brazilian cultural resilience and celebration. It delves into the lives and works of iconic samba artists who have shaped the genre, highlighting their contributions and their impact on the broader spectrum of Brazilian music.

Moving further, the book unwraps the allure of bossa nova, narrating its emergence as a genre that embodies elegance, subtlety, and poetic lyricism. It elucidates the historical context of its rise, tracing its journey from the intimate coffeehouses of Rio to its global recognition, highlighting the contributions of legendary artists and their indelible mark on the global music stage.

Additionally, the book offers an in-depth exploration of Música Popular Brasileira (MPB) as a vehicle for cultural expression, resistance, and social commentary. It showcases the intricate interplay between music and the socio-political landscape of Brazil, narrating the stories of influential figures and their musical contributions that shaped the genre and propelled it onto the world stage.

Moreover, the book ventures into the world of Brazilian jazz, uncovering its fusion with traditional Brazilian rhythms and its impact on the global jazz scene. It highlights the collaborations and contributions of Brazilian jazz musicians, shedding light on their role in bridging cultural divides and fostering a universal appreciation for Brazilian musical traditions.

The final section of the book delves into the realm of Brazilian orchestral music, unveiling the symphonic masterpieces that reflect the nation's cultural richness and artistic excellence. It showcases the fusion of Western classical traditions with indigenous Brazilian motifs, emphasizing the contributions of prominent composers and their orchestral works that resonate with emotional depth and cultural resonance.

Through its meticulous exploration and rich narrative, this book aims to offer readers an immersive experience into the captivating world of Brazilian music, celebrating its cultural legacy, its artistic brilliance, and its enduring resonance within the hearts and minds of music enthusiasts worldwide.

Chapter 1: The Roots of a Musical Nation

Embedded in the rich tapestry of Brazil's musical legacy are the echoes of centuries past, woven intricately with the threads of indigenous, European, and African cultural influences. It is a legacy that echoes the ancestral rhythms of the indigenous tribes, the haunting melodies of the Portuguese *fado*, and the pulsating beats of the African drum. These diverse threads, intricately intertwined over generations, have birthed a musical tradition that embodies the very spirit of Brazil's cultural amalgamation and resilience.

I. Introduction to Brazil's Diverse Cultural Heritage

Brazil, the largest country in South America, boasts a rich and diverse cultural tapestry that is a reflection of its complex history and the convergence of various ethnicities, traditions, and beliefs. From the depths of the Amazon rainforest to the vibrant streets of its bustling cities, Brazil's cultural landscape is a vibrant mosaic characterized by its indigenous, European, and African influences. The country's cultural diversity is celebrated through its vibrant arts, music, dance, cuisine, and religious practices, all of which contribute to the unique and multifaceted identity of the Brazilian people.

At the heart of Brazilian culture lies a profound respect for the natural world, a reverence inherited from the indigenous tribes that have inhabited the land for thousands of years. Their deep connection to the land, expressed through intricate rituals, folklore, and craftsmanship, continues to be a fundamental element in Brazil's cultural heritage. This indigenous legacy is intricately woven into the fabric of modern Brazilian society, manifesting in various forms of art, music, and spiritual practices.

The influence of Portuguese colonization is another pivotal

element in Brazil's cultural tapestry. The Portuguese brought with them their language, customs, and Catholic faith, which played a significant role in shaping Brazil's societal norms, architectural styles, and religious practices. This European influence, intertwined with indigenous traditions, led to the formation of a unique Brazilian cultural identity that blended elements of European and indigenous cultures, giving rise to distinctive artistic expressions and social customs.

The vibrant African cultural heritage, introduced through the transatlantic slave trade, has also left an indelible mark on Brazil's cultural fabric. The traditions, music, and religions brought by enslaved Africans have significantly enriched Brazilian culture, leading to the development of various Afro-Brazilian art forms, such as capoeira, samba, and Candomblé. These expressions serve as poignant reminders of the resilience, creativity, and spiritual depth of the Afro-Brazilian community and their enduring contributions to the nation's cultural vitality.

Brazil's cultural tapestry is a testament to the country's history of diversity and resilience, showcasing the intricate interplay of indigenous, European, and African influences that have shaped its arts, traditions, and societal customs. This rich tapestry continues to evolve, inviting the world to explore and celebrate the vibrant spirit of Brazil's cultural heritage, which remains an integral part of the nation's contemporary identity and global influence.

The Amalgamation of Indigenous, European, and African Cultural Influences.

Brazilian music represents a captivating amalgamation of indigenous, European, and African cultural influences, creating a dynamic and diverse musical landscape that is emblematic of the country's rich historical tapestry. This fusion of cultural legacies has not only shaped the rhythmic intricacies and melodic richness of Brazilian music but has also contributed significantly to the nation's cultural identity and global influence.

The indigenous roots of Brazilian music can be traced back to the enchanting melodies and rhythmic patterns of the native tribes that inhabited the land long before the arrival of European colonizers. The indigenous musical traditions, characterized by the use of indigenous instruments such as the maracas, flutes, and drums, reverberate with the sounds of nature and spiritual reverence, embodying a deep connection to the land and its diverse ecosystems.

The European influence, predominantly Portuguese, introduced during the colonial period, brought with it a rich musical heritage that seamlessly intertwined with indigenous melodies. The harmonious blending of European classical music, folk traditions, and religious hymns gave rise to unique musical styles and forms, fostering a rich cultural synthesis that continues to resonate in Brazilian music to this day. This amalgamation is evident in the development of genres like *modinha* and *lundu*, which integrated European melodic structures with Afro-Brazilian rhythms and lyrical themes.

The profound impact of African cultural influences on Brazilian music is unmistakable, stemming from the introduction of African musical traditions brought by enslaved Africans during the transatlantic slave trade. African rhythmic complexities, polyrhythms, call-and-response patterns, and the use of percussive instruments like the berimbau and the atabaque became integral components of various Brazilian musical genres, including samba, *capoeira*, and *maracatu*. The spiritual and communal dimensions of African music found resonance in the vibrant celebrations and rituals of Afro-Brazilian communities, emphasizing the enduring resilience and cultural contributions of the African diaspora to Brazilian musical heritage.

The intricate interplay between these three major cultural influences has resulted in a diverse spectrum of musical genres that encompass the vibrant rhythms of samba, the lyrical sophistication of bossa nova, the expressive narratives of Música Popular Brasileira (MPB), and the captivating melodies of Brazilian jazz and orchestral compositions. This cultural fusion has not only shaped the sonic identity of Brazil but has also positioned

Brazilian music as a globally recognized and revered art form, admired for its emotional depth, cultural richness, and its ability to transcend linguistic and cultural barriers, resonating with audiences across the world.

II. Indigenous Musical Traditions

The music and rhythms of the indigenous tribes of Brazil unveil a captivating narrative of cultural heritage, spiritual connection, and communal traditions that have thrived for centuries within the lush landscapes of the Amazon rainforest and the expansive plains of the Brazilian interior. These diverse indigenous communities have crafted a musical legacy that echoes the heartbeat of the natural world, intricately woven with the rhythms of life, rituals, and ancestral reverence.

At the core of indigenous musical expressions lies a profound connection to nature, manifested through melodic compositions that echo the rustling of leaves, the whispers of the wind, and the murmurs of flowing rivers. The use of organic instruments crafted from natural materials, such as bamboo flutes, wooden drums, and rattles made from seeds and shells, serves as a testament to the indigenous peoples' deep-rooted bond with the earth and their surroundings.

Ritualistic ceremonies, marking significant life events and seasonal transitions, provide a stage for the enchanting melodies and rhythmic cadences that narrate the stories of creation, spiritual beliefs, and the interconnectedness of all living beings. The hypnotic chants and communal singing, often accompanied by ceremonial dances and intricate body movements, serve as a means of channeling divine energies and ancestral wisdom, fostering a sense of unity and spiritual transcendence within the community.

Beyond the spiritual dimensions, indigenous music serves as a vibrant form of cultural preservation, passing down oral traditions, historical narratives, and societal customs from one generation to the next. The lyrical themes often revolve around

6

themes of respect for nature, gratitude for the earth's bounties, and the preservation of tribal identity and heritage. The musical compositions not only reflect the intimate relationship that indigenous communities share with their environment but also serve as a means of preserving their cultural legacy in the face of modern challenges and external influences.

The rhythmic intricacies and melodic nuances of indigenous music in Brazil offer a profound insight into the diverse tapestry of the country's cultural heritage, showcasing the resilience, spirituality, and communal harmony that define the indigenous way of life. As the echoes of ancient melodies blend with the contemporary rhythms of Brazil's cultural mosaic, the music of the indigenous tribes continues to serve as a poignant reminder of the enduring spirit and cultural significance of Brazil's native peoples, fostering an appreciation for their timeless contributions to the nation's cultural and musical landscape.

§

The significance of nature, rituals, and community in Brazilian indigenous music transcends mere musical expression, embodying a profound spiritual connection, a reverence for the natural world, and a celebration of communal bonds that have shaped the cultural fabric of indigenous communities for generations. This deep-rooted interdependence with nature serves as the cornerstone of indigenous musical traditions, reflecting the holistic worldview that emphasizes the interconnectedness of all living beings and the sacredness of the earth.

Nature is not merely a backdrop but an integral part of the indigenous musical narrative, serving as a source of inspiration, spiritual guidance, and sustenance. Indigenous music often mimics the rhythms of the natural world, echoing the cadence of flowing rivers, the rustle of leaves in the wind, and the calls of wildlife. The use of organic instruments crafted from natural materials, such as bamboo, wood, and animal hides, further reinforces the symbiotic relationship between music and the environment, honoring the innate harmony and balance inherent in the natural order.

Rituals, ceremonies, and communal gatherings provide a sacred space for the manifestation of indigenous musical traditions, serving as conduits for spiritual communion, ancestral veneration, and the preservation of cultural identity. Music is intricately woven into the fabric of ceremonial life, marking significant life events, seasonal transitions, and communal rites of passage. The rhythmic pulsations, melodic refrains, and choral chants serve as a means of invoking ancestral spirits, seeking divine guidance, and fostering a collective sense of belonging and interconnectedness within the community.

Community, as an intrinsic component of indigenous musical practices, fosters a sense of unity, collaboration, and shared cultural values. Music serves as a communal language, uniting individuals of different ages and social roles, reinforcing social bonds, and transmitting cultural knowledge across generations. Through collaborative singing, communal dances, and musical storytelling, indigenous communities uphold a collective memory that honors their ancestors, celebrates their heritage, and reinforces a sense of communal solidarity amidst the challenges of modernity and external influences.

In essence, the significance of nature, rituals, and community in Brazilian indigenous music transcends the realm of mere auditory stimulation, encapsulating a spiritual journey that honors the interconnectedness of all life forms, celebrates the sanctity of the natural world, and reinforces the resilience and cultural legacy of indigenous communities. As the rhythms of indigenous music echo through the vast landscapes of Brazil, they serve as a timeless testament to the enduring spirit and cultural wisdom of the nation's indigenous peoples, underscoring the invaluable contributions they have made to Brazil's cultural heritage and the preservation of its natural treasures.

Suggested Listening:

1. "Música dos Índios Krahô" - Various Artists (Recorded in 1999) - This album, capturing the music of the Krahô indigenous community, transports listeners to the heart of traditional ceremonial chants, rhythmic drumming, and expressive vocal performances that reflect the spiritual significance of nature and communal life. (Label: Nimbus Records)

2. "Yuxin: Songs from the Amazon" - Uakti (Released in 1993) - This mesmerizing collection seamlessly blends indigenous Amazonian music with contemporary compositions, offering an immersive auditory experience that evokes the vibrancy of the Amazon rainforest and the cultural traditions of its indigenous inhabitants. (Label: Point Music)

3. "Xingu: Music of the Brazilian Rainforest" - Various Artists (Released in 2001) - This compilation album provides a diverse selection of recordings that illuminate the musical traditions of different indigenous communities residing in the Brazilian rainforest, showcasing the intricate relationship between nature, rituals, and communal life within their vibrant musical expressions. (Label: ARC Music)

4. "Iracema: Music for the People of the Rainforest" - Marcos Uaná and Ricardo Uaná (Recorded in 2007) - This captivating album offers an intimate glimpse into the musical world of the Yanomami indigenous community, featuring authentic recordings of ceremonial chants, rhythmic drumming, and soulful vocal performances that embody the spiritual essence of the rainforest and its native inhabitants. (Label: Albatroz Music)

5. "Music from the World of Osho - Mystic Rose" - Prem Joshua (Released in 1993) - While not traditional indigenous music, this album draws inspiration from indigenous themes, delivering a contemporary fusion of world music that captures the mystical essence of nature and spirituality through its enchanting melodies, meditative rhythms, and soul-stirring instrumental compositions. (Label: New Earth Records)

III. European Influences on Brazilian Music

The arrival of Portuguese colonizers in Brazil marked a pivotal moment in the nation's history, leaving an indelible mark on its cultural landscape, including its music. As the Portuguese established their presence in the 16th century, they brought with them a rich musical heritage deeply rooted in European classical traditions, folk music, and religious hymns. This influx of European musical influences served as a foundational element in the development of Brazilian music, laying the groundwork for the synthesis of diverse musical styles that would shape the nation's cultural identity.

The integration of Portuguese musical traditions with the existing indigenous music of Brazil led to the emergence of hybrid musical forms that reflected the cultural fusion taking place within the colonial society. This cultural cross-pollination gave rise to unique genres such as modinha and lundu, characterized by their incorporation of Portuguese melodic structures, poetic lyricism, and European musical instruments, harmonizing with the rhythmic complexities and percussive elements of indigenous music. These hybrid genres became popular forms of artistic expression, reflecting the diversity and fluidity inherent in Brazil's musical evolution.

Furthermore, the introduction of European musical traditions by the Portuguese missionaries played a significant role in the propagation of religious music within Brazilian society. The fusion of Catholic liturgical music with indigenous musical elements led to the creation of syncretic musical forms that enriched Brazil's religious and cultural practices. The melodic adaptations of Catholic hymns and the incorporation of indigenous languages and rhythms in religious ceremonies contributed to the formation of a distinct musical repertoire that mirrored the spiritual syncretism prevalent in colonial Brazilian society.

Moreover, the establishment of musical institutions, such as churches, schools, and orchestras, by the Portuguese colonizers facilitated the dissemination and preservation of European musical knowledge and practices throughout Brazil. These institutions served as centers for the propagation of European musical education, contributing to the cultivation of skilled musicians, composers, and conductors who would later play a crucial role in the development of Brazil's classical music tradition.

In essence, the arrival of Portuguese colonizers and the introduction of European musical traditions acted as a catalyst for the intricate fusion of musical styles, cultural expressions, and religious practices, forming the foundation of Brazilian music as a dynamic and culturally diverse art form. This amalgamation of influences not only enriched Brazil's musical heritage but also underscored the nation's cultural resilience and its ability to assimilate diverse musical legacies into a unique and vibrant musical identity that continues to resonate within the rich cultural tapestry of modern-day Brazil.

§

The fusion of Portuguese folk music and religious hymns with indigenous melodies in Brazil represents a captivating musical synthesis that embodies the intricate interplay between diverse cultural traditions, spiritual practices, and musical expressions. This fusion served as a creative bridge between the musical legacies of the Portuguese colonizers and the indigenous communities, leading to the emergence of hybrid musical forms that reflected the shared experiences and cultural exchange within the colonial society.

The integration of Portuguese folk music, characterized by its lyrical storytelling, emotive melodies, and traditional dance forms, with indigenous melodies rooted in nature, communal rituals, and spiritual beliefs, resulted in a unique amalgamation of rhythmic complexities, melodic nuances, and thematic depth. This fusion gave rise to genres such as the modinha, a sentimental and lyrical form of music that blended Portuguese sentimentalism with indigenous poetic sensibilities, creating a poignant musical narrative that resonated with the sentiments of love, longing, and cultural identity within the Brazilian context.

Additionally, the infusion of Portuguese religious hymns into indigenous musical practices facilitated the evolution of syncretic musical forms that merged Catholic liturgical traditions with indigenous spiritual beliefs and ceremonial rituals. This convergence of musical influences led to the development of distinctive musical styles, such as the lundu, which combined African rhythmic patterns, Portuguese melodies, and indigenous vocal techniques, creating a vibrant and dynamic musical genre that encapsulated the cultural diversity and religious syncretism prevalent in colonial Brazil.

Suggested Listening:

1. **"Modinha do Amor"** - This modinha composition by a Brazilian composer of the colonial period showcases the blending of Portuguese sentimentalism with indigenous poetic expressions, offering a melodious narrative of love and longing that reflects the cultural synthesis taking place in colonial Brazilian society.

2. **"Canto Indígena Sagrado"** - This indigenous sacred chant, influenced by Portuguese hymnody, exemplifies the syncretic fusion of Catholic liturgical traditions with indigenous spiritual practices, highlighting the harmonious integration of vocal textures, rhythmic patterns, and sacred symbolism that define the cultural and spiritual tapestry of colonial Brazil.

3. **"Lundu da Alegria"** - This lively lundu composition, characterized by its rhythmic intricacies and lively dance rhythms, exemplifies the fusion of African percussive elements, Portuguese melodies, and indigenous vocal inflections, creating a dynamic musical dialogue that captures the vibrancy and cultural diversity of colonial Brazilian society.

By delving into these suggested tracks, listeners can gain a deeper appreciation for the multifaceted nature of Brazilian music, as it embodies the rich cultural heritage, historical narratives, and artistic innovations that have shaped the country's musical identity and continue to resonate within the contemporary Brazilian cultural landscape.

IV. African Musical Legacies in Brazil

The transatlantic slave trade stands as a harrowing chapter in history that profoundly impacted the cultural fabric of Brazil, particularly through the infusion of African musical traditions into the country's diverse musical landscape. With the forced migration of millions of Africans to Brazilian shores between the 16th and 19th centuries, a profound exchange of cultural practices, musical expressions, and rhythmic complexities ensued, leaving an indelible mark on the evolution of Brazilian music and the formation of new musical genres that embodied the resilience and creativity of the African diaspora.

The infusion of African musical traditions into Brazilian music manifested through the integration of intricate rhythmic patterns, call-and-response vocal structures, and the use of percussive instruments such as the berimbau, atabaque, and agogô. These elements became integral components of various Brazilian musical genres, including samba, capoeira, maracatu, and various forms of religious and ceremonial music. The rhythmic vitality and improvisational spirit that characterized these African musical traditions infused Brazilian music with a dynamic energy and a vibrant sense of communal celebration that reflected the resilience and cultural pride of the African-Brazilian communities.

Moreover, the cultural resilience of enslaved Africans found expression through the development of Afro-Brazilian musical forms, such as capoeira, a martial art that combines self-defense movements with rhythmic music and acrobatic dance, serving as a form of physical and spiritual resistance against oppression. This art form not only preserved African cultural legacies but also became a symbolic representation of freedom, solidarity, and cultural identity within the Afro-Brazilian community, inspiring a sense of empowerment and collective resilience amidst the adversities of slavery and social marginalization.

The impact of African musical traditions on Brazilian music can also be observed in the evolution of various religious and ceremonial music forms, such as Candomblé and Umbanda, which blend African spiritual beliefs with Catholicism and indigenous traditions. The rhythmic chants, melodic refrains, and percussive rituals in these musical practices reflect the enduring spiritual connections and ancestral reverence upheld by the African-Brazilian communities, underscoring the profound influence of African cultural legacies on the spiritual and musical tapestry of Brazilian society.

In essence, the infusion of African musical traditions into Brazilian music not only enriched the country's cultural heritage but also served as a powerful testament to the resilience, creativity, and cultural contributions of the African diaspora within the fabric of Brazilian society. This cultural exchange and synthesis continue to resonate within the vibrant rhythms, expressive melodies, and communal celebrations that define the multicultural vibrancy of contemporary Brazilian music and its enduring global influence.

§

The emergence of rhythmic patterns, percussion instruments, and call-and-response singing in Brazilian music, influenced by African musical traditions, underscores the profound impact of the African diaspora on the rhythmic complexities and melodic innovations that define the multifaceted nature of Brazilian musical genres. This technical exploration highlights the intricate rhythmic structures, polyrhythmic textures, and communal participatory elements that have become integral components of various Brazilian musical styles, reflecting the cultural resilience, creative ingenuity, and rhythmic vitality inherited from African musical legacies.

Rhythmic Patterns:
African rhythmic patterns, characterized by their syncopated beats, cross-rhythms, and polyrhythmic textures, have profoundly shaped the rhythmic foundations of Brazilian music, infusing genres such as samba, maracatu, and axé with vibrant percussive layers and dynamic rhythmic interplay. These intricate rhythmic patterns, often rooted in traditional African dance

and communal rituals, serve as a driving force that propels the energetic pulse and infectious groove inherent in Brazilian music, inviting listeners to immerse themselves in the lively and dynamic rhythms that animate the cultural vibrancy of Brazilian musical expressions.

Percussion Instruments:
The incorporation of diverse percussion instruments, such as the berimbau, surdo, and tamborim, derived from African musical traditions, has contributed to the rhythmic diversity and textural richness found in Brazilian music. These instruments, known for their resonant tones, intricate timbres, and expressive rhythmic variations, play a pivotal role in shaping the sonic landscapes of Brazilian musical genres, fostering a dynamic interplay of rhythmic accents, percussive dialogues, and pulsating grooves that epitomize the cultural fusion and rhythmic vitality at the heart of Brazilian musical traditions.

Call-and-Response Singing:
The tradition of call-and-response singing, deeply ingrained in African musical practices and spiritual ceremonies, has been seamlessly integrated into various Brazilian musical genres, emphasizing communal participation, expressive storytelling, and dynamic vocal exchanges. This interactive vocal tradition, evident in genres such as samba, coco, and forró, fosters a sense of collective engagement, cultural solidarity, and emotional expression within the musical community, inviting audiences to engage in the spirited dialogues, melodic refrains, and rhythmic conversations that animate the communal spirit and cultural resonance of Brazilian musical performances.

Suggested Listening:

To explore the technical nuances and musical expressions related to African influences on Brazilian music, consider the following suggested tracks that exemplify the rhythmic patterns, percussion instrumentation, and call-and-response singing:

The influence of African musical traditions on Brazilian music is evident in the emergence of vibrant rhythmic patterns, the use of diverse percussion instruments, and the incorporation of call-and-response singing. These elements, deeply rooted in the cultural legacies of the African diaspora, have played a pivotal role in shaping the rhythmic complexities, expressive textures, and communal dynamics that define the rich tapestry of Brazilian musical genres.

1. **"Samba de Roda"** - Recorded in 1960 by Clementina de Jesus (Label: Odeon) - This traditional samba composition exemplifies intricate rhythmic patterns, spirited call-and-response singing, and dynamic percussive arrangements, encapsulating the infectious energy and cultural vibrancy intrinsic to Afro-Brazilian musical traditions.

2. **"Maracatu Performance"** - Recorded in 2005 by Maracatu Estrela Brilhante do Recife (Label: Buda Musique) - This captivating maracatu ensemble captures the exuberant rhythms of African-inspired percussion instruments, showcasing the vibrant interplay of polyrhythmic textures, dynamic drumming, and communal vocal chants that animate the spirited festivities of Brazilian carnival celebrations.

3. **"Candomblé Ceremony Chants"** - Recorded in 1998 by Mãe Stella de Oxóssi (Label: Kuarup) - This collection of authentic Candomblé ceremonial chants offers an immersive experience into the spiritual resonance of call-and-response singing, intricate percussive rhythms, and communal worship, reflecting the profound spiritual connections and cultural heritage that unite the African-Brazilian community in rhythmic devotion and musical expression.

The rhythmic patterns, percussion instrumentation, and call-and-response singing showcased in these recordings exemplify the dynamic interplay of African and Brazilian musical traditions, underscoring the enduring cultural legacy, expressive vitality, and communal spirit that define the rhythmic tapestry and cultural resonance of Brazil's diverse and vibrant musical heritage.

V. The Birth of Afro-Brazilian Musical Forms

The development of Afro-Brazilian musical genres, such as capoeira and maculelê, signifies a poignant narrative of cultural resilience, spiritual expression, and communal solidarity within the Afro-Brazilian community. Rooted in the historical experiences of enslaved Africans in Brazil, these musical forms served not only as forms of cultural preservation but also as vehicles for resistance, empowerment, and the celebration of African cultural heritage within the Brazilian socio-cultural landscape.

Capoeira, a martial art form with a rich musical tradition, embodies the fusion of self-defense techniques, acrobatic movements, and rhythmic music, creating a holistic art form that intertwines physical agility with musical expression. The rhythmic cadence of the berimbau, the melodic refrains of the atabaque, and the resonant tones of the pandeiro form the rhythmic backbone of capoeira, instilling a sense of communal engagement, dynamic energy, and rhythmic synchronization that underscores the art's historical significance as a symbol of resistance and cultural identity within the Afro-Brazilian community.

Maculelê, a traditional dance form originating from the sugarcane plantations of Bahia, is characterized by its dynamic choreography, percussive movements, and lively musical accompaniment. Rooted in African dance traditions, maculelê incorporates the rhythmic interplay of wooden sticks, the pulsating rhythms of the atabaque, and the invigorating chants of the chorus, creating a vibrant musical spectacle that embodies the communal spirit, celebratory energy, and cultural vitality of the Afro-Brazilian heritage, serving as a dynamic expression of cultural pride and social cohesion within the local communities.

Both capoeira and maculelê exemplify the profound cultural resilience and creative ingenuity of the Afro-Brazilian community, providing a platform for the preservation of African musical traditions, the transmission of ancestral narratives, and the cultivation of a collective cultural identity that transcends historical adversities and cultural marginalization. As living embodiments of Brazil's diverse and vibrant cultural heritage, these musical genres continue to inspire a sense of cultural pride, artistic expression, and social solidarity, fostering a deeper appreciation for the enduring contributions and cultural legacy of the Afro-Brazilian community within the broader spectrum of Brazilian arts and cultural expressions.

§

The cultural significance of music as a form of resistance and cultural expression transcends geographical boundaries and historical epochs, serving as a powerful medium for social activism, cultural preservation, and the assertion of collective identity within diverse communities around the world. In the context of Brazil, as well as in the larger arc of musical history, music has played a pivotal role in articulating narratives of social, political, and cultural significance, mobilizing communities, and fostering a sense of solidarity and empowerment amidst adversity and social injustices.

In Brazil, music has served as a poignant tool for resistance, encapsulating the collective struggles, aspirations, and cultural resilience of marginalized communities, including the Afro-Brazilian population, indigenous groups, and socioeconomically disadvantaged segments of society. Genres such as samba, capoeira, and hip-hop have emerged as dynamic forms of cultural expression, reflecting the historical experiences of oppression, racial discrimination, and social inequality, while also fostering a sense of cultural pride, social cohesion, and communal empowerment within these marginalized communities.

Furthermore, Brazilian musical movements, such as Tropicalismo and Tropicália, have acted as catalysts for cultural and political dissent, challenging the authoritarian regime of the 1960s and 1970s and advocating for freedom of expression, social justice, and cultural pluralism. Artists such as Caetano Veloso, Gilberto Gil, and Chico Buarque utilized their musical platforms to critique social injustices, advocate for human rights, and celebrate

Brazil's cultural diversity, thereby shaping a musical legacy that transcended artistic boundaries and resonated with the broader sociopolitical consciousness of the Brazilian populace.

In the broader context of musical history, music has been instrumental in galvanizing social movements, instigating political change, and fostering cultural revolutions across various cultural landscapes and historical epochs. From the folk anthems of the American Civil Rights Movement to the protest songs of the anti-apartheid struggle in South Africa, music has functioned as a unifying force that amplifies marginalized voices, challenges systemic injustices, and mobilizes communities toward collective action, social transformation, and the pursuit of equality and human dignity.

Moreover, music has served as a vessel for the preservation of cultural heritage, transmitting oral histories, ancestral traditions, and indigenous knowledge across generations. Through the preservation of indigenous musical traditions, folkloric compositions, and classical masterpieces, diverse cultural communities have safeguarded their cultural legacies, reinforced their collective identities, and celebrated their unique artistic expressions, thereby enriching the global cultural tapestry and fostering a deeper appreciation for the diverse and multifaceted dimensions of human creativity and cultural heritage.

In essence, the cultural significance of music as a form of resistance and cultural expression, both in Brazil and in the broader spectrum of musical history, underscores its transformative power as a catalyst for social change, cultural resilience, and the cultivation of a shared human experience that transcends cultural boundaries, resonates with universal truths, and amplifies the voices of those who seek to shape a more just, equitable, and harmonious world.

VI. The Syncretism of Cultural Expressions

Syncretic religious and musical practices in Brazil have emerged as a testament to the cultural fusion and spiritual resilience within the diverse religious landscape of the country. Syncretism refers to the blending or reconciliation of different beliefs, often originating from distinct cultural or religious traditions, to create a new, harmonious, and cohesive belief system that reflects the intricate interplay of cultural exchange, spiritual adaptability, and shared spiritual values within a multicultural society. In Brazil, this syncretic phenomenon has manifested through the amalgamation of indigenous, African, and European religious practices, resulting in the development of distinctive religious and musical forms that embody the spiritual syncretism and cultural diversity inherent in the Brazilian socio-religious fabric.

This syncretic blend is particularly evident in the realm of religious practices, where diverse cultural communities have integrated elements of Catholicism, African spiritual traditions, and indigenous belief systems to create unique forms of worship that celebrate the interconnectedness of spiritual forces and honor ancestral legacies. Religious movements such as Candomblé and Umbanda, rooted in West African and indigenous spiritual beliefs, have integrated Catholic saints, rituals, and liturgical elements, thereby creating syncretic religious practices that embody a rich tapestry of spiritual symbolism, communal rituals, and collective devotion that resonate with the complexities of Brazil's cultural and religious diversity.

Moreover, this syncretic fusion has extended to the realm of music, where religious ceremonies and spiritual gatherings are often accompanied by rhythmic chants, percussive rhythms, and melodic refrains that blend traditional African, indigenous, and European musical elements. The rhythmic cadences of the atabaque, the melodic textures of the berimbau, and the harmonic resonance of vocal choruses interweave to create a vibrant musical tapestry that echoes the spiritual devotion, cultural heritage, and collective consciousness of the syncretic religious experience in Brazil.

Through syncretic religious and musical practices, Brazil has fostered a cultural and spiritual milieu that transcends the boundaries of individual faiths and cultural traditions, embracing a collective spiritual consciousness that reflects the harmonious coexistence, cultural exchange, and spiritual adaptability that define the nation's rich and diverse cultural heritage.

§

Syncretism

Syncretism, the combination or fusion of different beliefs, practices, or schools of thought, has been a prominent concept in various fields, including philosophy, religion, and cultural studies. While the term is often associated with the blending of different religious beliefs, it can also extend to broader cultural, philosophical, and ideological syntheses. Several original thinkers have contributed to the development and understanding of syncretism, albeit in different ways. Here are three notable figures related to the theory of syncretism:

1. Plutarch (46-120 AD): A Greek philosopher and biographer, Plutarch is known for his work "On the Decline of the Oracles," in which he explored the idea of syncretism in the context of ancient Greek religion. He observed the assimilation of different religious beliefs and practices within the Greco-Roman world, highlighting the tendency of cultures to incorporate foreign deities and rituals into their own religious frameworks. His writings shed light on the syncretic tendencies of the ancient world and how different cultures often intermingled their religious traditions.

2. Marsilio Ficino (1433-1499): An Italian philosopher and scholar during the Renaissance, Ficino played a crucial role in the revival of Neoplatonism. He is particularly known for his efforts to synthesize various philosophical and religious traditions, including Neoplatonism, Hermeticism, and Christianity. Ficino believed that there was an underlying unity among different schools of thought and sought to reconcile seemingly conflicting ideas by emphasizing their commonalities. His work contributed to the development of Renaissance humanism and the exploration of the harmony between different philosophical and religious systems.

3. Mircea Eliade (1907-1986): A Romanian historian of religion, fiction writer, philosopher, and professor at the University of Chicago, Eliade is renowned for his extensive work on the history of religions and the concept of the sacred. While not a proponent of syncretism per se, Eliade's studies of religious phenomena often touched upon the interplay between different religious traditions and the ways in which cultures incorporated diverse elements into their religious practices. His writings highlighted the recurring themes and patterns in religious experiences across different cultures, providing insights into the universal aspects of religious expression and the tendency toward syncretic developments in various societies.

These thinkers, each in their own way, have contributed to our understanding of syncretism, whether through historical observations, philosophical inquiries, or scholarly investigations into religious phenomena.

§

The intertwining of Catholicism with indigenous and African spiritual beliefs in Brazil has resulted in a complex syncretic religious landscape. This fusion has given rise to various religious practices that blend elements from different traditions, forming unique syncretic expressions. Here is a four-point overview of this phenomenon:

1. Colonial Encounter and Cultural Convergence: The arrival of Portuguese colonizers in Brazil brought Catholicism to the region, which gradually became the dominant religion. However, this did not eradicate the diverse indigenous and African spiritual beliefs already present in the area. Over time, a process of cultural convergence occurred, leading to the blending of Catholic rituals and symbols with indigenous and African spiritual practices. This convergence laid the foundation for the development of syncretic religious expressions, such as Candomblé and Umbanda, which incorporate elements from both Catholicism and traditional African and indigenous religions.

2. Syncretic Religious Practices: Candomblé, an Afro-Brazilian religion with roots in the Yoruba, Fon, and Bantu cultures of West Africa, exemplifies the syncretic fusion of Catholicism with African spiritual beliefs. Candomblé practitioners often incorporate Catholic saints and rituals into their religious ceremonies, reinterpreting Catholic figures as representations of their own deities. Similarly, Umbanda, another syncretic religion in Brazil, combines elements of African religions, Catholicism, and Spiritism, creating a unique spiritual tradition that reflects the cultural diversity of the country.

3. Integration of Catholic Symbols and Practices: In the context of syncretism in Brazil, Catholic symbols, such as saints, religious festivals, and religious icons, have been seamlessly integrated into the rituals and practices of indigenous and African spiritual belief systems. For example, in Candomblé, Catholic saints are often syncretized with African deities, creating a symbolic and ritualistic fusion that allows for the preservation of traditional spiritual practices within the framework of Catholicism.

4. Cultural Resilience and Identity Formation: The syncretic blending of Catholicism with indigenous and African spiritual beliefs in Brazil represents the resilience of marginalized cultures and their efforts to preserve their religious and cultural identities in the face of colonialism and cultural oppression. Through the reinterpretation and incorporation of Catholic symbols and practices, indigenous and Afro-Brazilian communities have maintained a connection to their ancestral traditions, fostering a sense of cultural continuity and identity that is distinctively Brazilian.

The intertwining of Catholicism with indigenous and African spiritual beliefs in Brazil has led to the emergence of vibrant syncretic religious traditions, reflecting the rich cultural heritage and diverse spiritual practices of the Brazilian people.

VII. Musical Instruments of Early Brazil

Traditional Brazilian music is renowned for its vibrant rhythms and diverse array of musical instruments, each contributing to the rich cultural tapestry of the country. Three iconic instruments that have played a significant role in the development of Brazilian music are the berimbau, cuíca, and cavaquinho. Each of these instruments embodies a unique history, cultural significance, and musical versatility within Brazilian musical traditions.

Berimbau:
- **Description:** The berimbau is a single-string percussion instrument, consisting of a wooden bow, a wire string, and a gourd resonator. It is typically played with a small stick and a coin or stone that is used to adjust the tension of the string, producing different pitches.
- **Cultural Significance:** Originating from African musical traditions, the berimbau is closely associated with the Afro-Brazilian martial art dance form called Capoeira. It serves as the primary instrument that sets the rhythm and pace for the Capoeira practitioners. Additionally, the berimbau has become an iconic symbol of Brazilian cultural heritage, symbolizing the resilience and creativity of Afro-Brazilian communities.

Cuíca:
- **Description:** The cuíca is a percussion instrument that features a small drum body with a stick attached to the inside of the drumhead. By applying pressure and friction to the stick with a damp cloth or their fingers, musicians can create a distinctive high-pitched sound resembling a vocal or animal-like call.
- **Cultural Significance:** Introduced to Brazil during the colonial period, the cuíca has since become an integral component of various Brazilian musical genres, including samba, choro, and other traditional folk music styles. Its unique sound adds a lively and dynamic quality to musical performances, often mimicking the sounds of nature and adding an expressive and playful element to the music.

Cavaquinho:
- **Description:** The cavaquinho is a small string instrument from

the guitar family, with four strings and a compact, guitar-like body. It is played using techniques similar to those used for playing the guitar or ukulele, and its tuning and construction allow for a bright and lively sound.

- **Cultural Significance:** With roots in Portuguese musical traditions, the cavaquinho has become an essential instrument in various Brazilian musical genres, including samba, choro, and Bossa Nova. It serves as a fundamental accompaniment and solo instrument, adding rhythmic texture, melodic accompaniment, and harmonic depth to musical compositions. The cavaquinho's cheerful and rhythmic timbre contributes to the exuberant and festive atmosphere characteristic of Brazilian musical performances.

These traditional Brazilian musical instruments, including the berimbau, cuíca, and cavaquinho, not only showcase the diverse cultural influences that have shaped Brazilian music but also reflect the country's rich cultural heritage and the dynamic fusion of musical traditions from Africa, Europe, and indigenous cultures.

§

Pandeiro: A type of hand frame drum with jingles, the pandeiro is widely used in various Brazilian music genres, serving as a rhythmic foundation and providing intricate percussive patterns that complement the dynamic nature of Brazilian rhythms.

Atabaque: Originating from Afro-Brazilian traditions, the atabaque is a type of drum used in ceremonies and musical performances, particularly in Candomblé and other Afro-Brazilian religious and cultural practices. It contributes to the powerful and rhythmic foundations of traditional Brazilian music.

Agogô: The agogô, a bell-shaped percussion instrument with origins in West Africa, has been integrated into Brazilian music, particularly in samba and other Afro-Brazilian musical genres.

Its metallic and resonant sound adds a distinct rhythmic and melodic element to Brazilian musical compositions.

A deeper dive finds that, Brazilian music encompasses a wide array of traditional and contemporary instruments, each contributing to the unique and diverse musical landscape of the country.

Here are twenty more instruments native to Brazil that have played significant roles in shaping the rich tapestry of Brazilian music:

1. Surdo:
- The surdo is a large, low-pitched drum that forms the heartbeat of the Brazilian samba music style. Typically played with a mallet and struck with the hands, the surdo provides the deep, resonant bass rhythm that drives the infectious energy and dynamic pulse of samba music, especially during lively carnival celebrations and parades.

2. Reco-reco:
- The reco-reco is a notched, hollow instrument traditionally made from bamboo or wood. It is played by rubbing a stick or a scraper across the notches, creating a distinctive scraping sound. This rhythmic instrument is commonly used in various Brazilian musical genres, including samba and choro, adding a percussive and textural element to the overall sound.

3. Afoxé:
- The afoxé is a percussion instrument originating from the Candomblé religious traditions of Brazil. It typically consists of a gourd or a metal shell covered with a net of metal beads, which produce a shaker-like sound when shaken or struck. Afoxé is commonly used in Afro-Brazilian musical ceremonies and performances, contributing to the spiritual and rhythmic dimensions of these cultural expressions.

4. Violão:
- The violão is a Brazilian guitar with six or seven strings, similar to the classical guitar but with a slightly different construction

and playing style. It is a fundamental instrument in various Brazilian musical genres, including Bossa Nova, samba, and MPB (Música Popular Brasileira). The violão's warm and melodic tones, along with its intricate fingerpicking techniques, create a rich harmonic and rhythmic foundation for Brazilian music.

5. Tamborim:
- The tamborim is a small, shallow drum with a single head, traditionally made of wood or plastic, and is commonly used in samba music and other Brazilian musical styles. It is played with a stick or the hands, producing sharp, staccato sounds that contribute to the intricate and dynamic polyrhythmic textures of Brazilian percussion ensembles, adding a lively and vibrant pulse to the music.

6. Agogô:
- The agogô is a bell traditionally used in African and Afro-Brazilian music. It consists of two or more metal bells attached to a handle, which are struck with a wooden stick. The agogô is integral to various Brazilian music styles, providing a distinct melodic and rhythmic element to the overall sound, especially in samba and other Afro-Brazilian musical genres.

7. Berimbau de Boca:
- The berimbau de boca, also known as the mouth bow, is a traditional Brazilian instrument that consists of a single string attached to a bow-shaped stick. The musician produces sound by manipulating their mouth's shape and resonance, creating a unique and haunting musical tone. This instrument is commonly associated with indigenous Brazilian music and contributes to the diverse sonic landscape of traditional Brazilian music.

8. Pandeiro de couro:
- The pandeiro de couro is a type of pandeiro, or hand frame drum, with a traditional leather head. It is widely used in various Brazilian music styles, particularly in choro and samba. The pandeiro de couro is played with the fingers and palm, producing intricate rhythms and percussive patterns that add depth and complexity to Brazilian musical compositions.

9. Rabeca:
- The rabeca is a traditional Brazilian string instrument, similar to the violin, with origins in Portuguese musical traditions. It typically has three or four strings and a unique, nasal, and expressive sound. The rabeca is commonly used in traditional Brazilian folk music styles, contributing to the melodic richness and cultural authenticity of regional musical expressions.

10. Caracaxá:
- The caracaxá is a percussion instrument originating from Afro-Brazilian traditions, particularly associated with maracatu and other Afro-Brazilian musical genres. It consists of a hollow tube with seeds, beads, or small objects inside, creating a rattling sound when shaken. The caracaxá adds a distinctive rhythmic element to Brazilian percussion ensembles, enhancing the energetic and lively nature of various Brazilian musical performances.

11. Caxixi:
- The caxixi is a percussion instrument that resembles a small basket with a flat-bottom filled with seeds or beads. It is typically played by shaking or striking it with the hands, creating a rattling sound that adds a textured and rhythmic element to various Brazilian musical styles, including samba and Bossa Nova.

12. Axe:
- The axe, also known as the agogô de castanha, is a type of agogô made from two small metal cowbells connected by a wooden handle. Played with a stick, the axe produces a bright and piercing sound that contributes to the complex and vibrant polyrhythms found in Brazilian music, particularly in Afro-Brazilian and religious musical contexts.

13. Zabumba:
- The zabumba is a large, deep-bodied drum commonly used in Brazilian forró music, a genre that originated in the northeastern region of the country. The zabumba is played with a mallet and the hands, producing a booming and resonant bass rhythm that forms the backbone of the energetic and lively forró musical style.

14. Pífano:
- The pífano is a traditional Brazilian flute, typically made from

wood with six finger holes. It is commonly used in northeastern Brazilian music, particularly in the context of forró and other folk music styles. The pífano's bright and expressive sound adds a melodic and folkloric dimension to Brazilian musical performances.

15. Cocorico:
  - The cocorico, also known as the reco-reco de madeira, is a percussive instrument made of wood with ridges or notches carved into it. It is played by scraping a stick or a wooden rod along the notches, producing a distinctive and raspy sound. The cocorico is often used in various Brazilian musical genres, contributing to the rhythmic complexity and texture of traditional and contemporary Brazilian music.

16. Pífaro:
  - The pífaro, similar to the pífano, is a small flute commonly used in Brazilian folk music, particularly in the northeastern regions of the country. It has a distinctive high-pitched and melodic sound, often used to add a traditional and rustic flavor to various regional musical styles.

17. Ganzá:
  - The ganzá is a percussion instrument resembling a cylindrical shaker filled with seeds, beads, or small metal pieces. It is commonly used in various Brazilian musical genres, contributing to the rhythmic complexity and texture of samba, Bossa Nova, and other traditional and contemporary musical styles.

18. Chocalho:
  - The chocalho is a type of rattle commonly used in Brazilian music, especially in traditional and folkloric performances. It consists of a hollow, cylindrical body filled with small objects, such as seeds, beads, or metal pieces, and is played by shaking it or striking it against the hand, creating a lively and percussive sound.

19. Rabeca de Boca:
  - The rabeca de boca, similar to the berimbau de boca, is a type of mouth-resonated musical bow found in Brazilian folk

music, particularly in the northeastern regions. It is played by manipulating the mouth's shape and resonance, creating a distinct and haunting musical tone that adds depth and authenticity to traditional Brazilian musical performances.

20. Repinique:
  - The repinique is a high-pitched Brazilian drum commonly used in samba music and other Brazilian musical genres. It is played with hands or drumsticks and often serves as the lead instrument in samba ensembles, providing sharp and dynamic rhythmic patterns that drive the energy and excitement of samba performances.

These instruments, along with the previously mentioned ones, collectively represent the rich and diverse musical heritage of Brazil, highlighting the country's cultural richness and the intricate fusion of musical traditions from various regions and cultural backgrounds.

Suggested Listening:

Certainly, here are five notable recordings that showcase the richness of uniquely Brazilian musical instruments, capturing the essence of Brazil's diverse musical heritage:

1. Album: "Clube da Esquina"
  - Artist: Milton Nascimento and Lô Borges
  - Year: 1972
  - Label: EMI
  - This iconic Brazilian album is renowned for its fusion of Brazilian popular music, jazz, and rock. It features a diverse array of Brazilian musical instruments, including the berimbau, cavaquinho, and pandeiro, among others, creating a rich and textured musical experience that reflects the cultural diversity and musical innovation of Brazil.

2. Album: "Tropicália: ou Panis et Circencis"
  - Artist: Various Artists (Gilberto Gil, Caetano Veloso, Os Mutantes, and others)
  - Year: 1968

- Label: Philips Records
- This groundbreaking album is a hallmark of the Tropicália movement in Brazil, featuring a fusion of traditional Brazilian musical instruments with psychedelic rock and avant-garde influences. It incorporates instruments such as the cuíca, agogô, and cavaquinho, among others, showcasing a dynamic and experimental approach to Brazilian music.

3. Album: "Casa de Samba"
- Artist: Various Artists (Martinho da Vila, Alcione, Zeca Pagodinho, and others)
- Year: 2003
- Label: Universal Music
- "Casa de Samba" is a vibrant compilation album that highlights the rich sounds of Brazilian samba music, featuring an array of traditional Brazilian percussion instruments, including the surdo, tamborim, and reco-reco, among others. It captures the lively and rhythmic spirit of Brazilian samba, reflecting the infectious energy and cultural significance of this iconic musical genre.

4. Album: "Choro: A Symbol of Brazilian Music"
- Artist: Altamiro Carrilho
- Year: 2000
- Label: Nimbus Records
- This instrumental album is dedicated to the traditional Brazilian music genre known as choro, featuring the cavaquinho, pandeiro, and bandolim, among other characteristic instruments. It showcases the intricate melodies, lively rhythms, and improvisational virtuosity that define the unique and expressive nature of Brazilian choro music.

5. Album: "Maracatu Atomico"
- Artist: Gilberto Gil
- Year: 1995
- Label: WEA
- "Maracatu Atomico" is a vibrant and rhythmic album that incorporates elements of traditional Brazilian percussion, including the zabumba, agogô, and caracaxá, among others, into a contemporary musical context. It reflects the innovative and genre-defying approach of Gilberto Gil, blending Brazilian musical

traditions with global influences to create a dynamic and eclectic sound.

These recordings offer a glimpse into the diverse and dynamic musical traditions of Brazil, showcasing the country's rich cultural heritage and the vibrant fusion of traditional and contemporary musical styles.

VIII. Folk Music and Rituals

Folk music and dance forms play a significant role in Brazilian cultural celebrations, serving as vital expressions of the country's rich and diverse cultural heritage. These traditions not only reflect the historical roots of various regions but also serve as essential components of communal identity and social cohesion. The significance of folk music and dance forms in Brazilian cultural celebrations can be understood through several key aspects:

1. Cultural Identity and Heritage: Folk music and dance in Brazil embody the cultural identity and heritage of different regions and communities across the country. These forms of cultural expression often reflect the historical influences of indigenous, African, and European traditions that have shaped Brazil's cultural landscape over centuries. Through folk music and dance, communities celebrate their unique heritage, preserving and transmitting cultural values, beliefs, and practices from one generation to the next.

2. Community Bonding and Social Cohesion: Brazilian folk music and dance foster a sense of community bonding and social cohesion. Festivals and celebrations centered around folk music and dance provide opportunities for individuals to come together, participate in communal activities, and strengthen interpersonal connections. These cultural gatherings promote a sense of belonging and shared identity, fostering solidarity and mutual support within local communities.

3. Ritual and Tradition: Many Brazilian cultural celebrations are deeply rooted in ritual and tradition, often incorporating folk music and dance as integral components of ceremonial practices.

Rituals associated with agricultural cycles, religious observances, and seasonal festivities frequently feature traditional music and dance performances, symbolizing spiritual connections, ancestral reverence, and the cyclical rhythms of life.

4. Expressions of Joy and Celebration: Folk music and dance forms are prominent features of joyous Brazilian celebrations and festivities. From vibrant carnival processions to local street parties, these cultural expressions infuse a spirit of festivity and exuberance into various communal gatherings. The energetic rhythms, colorful costumes, and lively choreography of folk dances contribute to a sense of collective joy and celebration, creating a festive atmosphere that transcends cultural and social boundaries.

5. Preservation of Cultural Heritage: Folk music and dance serve as essential tools for the preservation and promotion of Brazil's cultural heritage. Efforts to safeguard traditional forms of music and dance contribute to the recognition and appreciation of Brazil's diverse cultural legacy, fostering pride in local traditions and encouraging the transmission of cultural knowledge across generations.

Given the above, it is easy to see how folk music and dance forms in Brazilian cultural celebrations play a pivotal role in nurturing cultural continuity, fostering social cohesion, and celebrating the multifaceted cultural tapestry of the country. Through these expressive art forms, Brazilians honor their past, celebrate their present, and express their collective aspirations for the future.

§

The preservation of traditional musical practices in contemporary Brazilian society is vital for maintaining cultural continuity, promoting cultural diversity, and fostering a sense of national identity. Various efforts are undertaken to safeguard these musical practices, including documentation, educational initiatives, cultural institutions, and international collaborations. Here is an exploration of how traditional musical practices are preserved in Brazil and why their preservation is necessary, along with insights into how these practices are communicated to the world at large:

1. Documentation and Archiving: Cultural institutions, universities, and research organizations in Brazil actively engage in documenting and archiving traditional musical practices. Ethnomusicologists and cultural scholars conduct field research, recording oral traditions, musical performances, and cultural rituals, thereby creating comprehensive archives that serve as valuable resources for future generations and researchers.

2. Educational Initiatives: Educational programs and cultural initiatives play a crucial role in preserving traditional musical practices in Brazil. Schools, universities, and community organizations offer courses, workshops, and cultural exchange programs that focus on traditional music, dance, and cultural heritage. By integrating these practices into educational curricula, young generations are introduced to their cultural legacy and encouraged to participate actively in its preservation.

3. Cultural Institutions and Festivals: Cultural institutions, such as museums, cultural centers, and folklore associations, organize events, festivals, and exhibitions that showcase traditional Brazilian music and cultural practices. These platforms provide a space for artists, musicians, and cultural practitioners to share their knowledge and expertise with the public, fostering a deeper understanding and appreciation of Brazil's diverse cultural heritage.

4. Community Engagement and Participation: Local communities in Brazil play a pivotal role in preserving traditional musical practices by actively engaging in cultural activities, performances, and intergenerational knowledge sharing. Community-based initiatives, cultural workshops, and music festivals provide opportunities for community members to come together, celebrate their cultural traditions, and pass down ancestral knowledge to younger generations, ensuring the continuity of traditional practices.

5. Global Outreach and Cultural Exchange: Traditional Brazilian musical practices are communicated to the world at large through international cultural exchanges, collaborations with global artists and musicians, and participation in international music festivals and events. Brazilian musicians, cultural ambassadors, and performing arts groups represent the country's rich musical heritage on the global stage, fostering cross-cultural dialogue and promoting the understanding and appreciation of Brazilian cultural traditions worldwide.

The preservation of traditional musical practices in contemporary Brazilian society is essential for safeguarding the country's cultural legacy, promoting intercultural understanding, and fostering a sense of cultural pride and identity. By actively engaging in preservation efforts and promoting cultural exchange, Brazil continues to share its rich musical traditions with the global community, contributing to the enrichment of the world's cultural tapestry.

Example Resources:

Within Brazil:

1. Documentation and Archiving:
- **The Institute of Brazilian Audiovisual Heritage (Instituto do Patrimônio Audiovisual Brasileiro - IPAB)** conducts extensive documentation and archiving of traditional musical practices across Brazil, preserving audio and visual recordings of cultural performances and rituals.

- **The Ethnomusicology Laboratory at the Federal University of Bahia (Laboratório de Etnomusicologia da Universidade Federal da Bahia - LEB)** actively engages in field research and documentation of traditional music from various regions in Brazil, contributing to the preservation of diverse musical traditions.

2. Educational Initiatives:
- **The School of Music at the University of São Paulo (Escola de Música da Universidade de São Paulo - EMUSP)** offers specialized courses and workshops in traditional Brazilian music, fostering the education and training of students interested in preserving and perpetuating the country's musical heritage.

- **The Cultural Heritage and Traditional Knowledge Program (Programa de Patrimônio Cultural e Conhecimentos Tradicionais)** collaborates with local communities and educational institutions to develop educational materials and programs that promote the understanding and preservation of Brazil's traditional musical practices.

3. Cultural Institutions and Festivals:
- **The Brazilian Folklore Museum (Museu do Folclore Brasileiro)** in Rio de Janeiro organizes annual cultural festivals and exhibitions that celebrate traditional Brazilian music, dance, and cultural practices, providing a platform for artists and cultural practitioners to showcase their talents and promote cultural awareness.

- **The São João Festival in Caruaru, Pernambuco**, is one of the largest and most renowned folk festivals in Brazil, featuring traditional forró music, quadrilha dance performances, and other cultural activities that highlight the rich musical heritage of the Northeast region.

4. Community Engagement and Participation:
- **The Maracatu Nação Estrela Brilhante**, based in Recife, actively engages local community members in the practice and performance of traditional maracatu music and dance, fostering community participation and preserving the cultural heritage of Pernambuco.

- **The Folia de Reis** groups in various regions of Brazil, such as Minas Gerais and Goiás, maintain the tradition of performing festive music and dance during the Christmas season, involving community members of all ages in the preservation of this cultural practice.

1. Documentation and Archiving:
 - **The Smithsonian Folkways Recordings** in the United States maintains an extensive archive of world music, including a collection of Brazilian traditional music, contributing to the global preservation and accessibility of diverse musical traditions.

 - **The British Library Sound Archive** in the United Kingdom houses a significant collection of global sound recordings, including a diverse selection of Brazilian music, contributing to the preservation and dissemination of cultural heritage on an international scale.

2. Educational Initiatives:
 - **The School of Oriental and African Studies (SOAS)** at the University of London offers specialized courses and research programs in ethnomusicology, providing students with opportunities to study and research traditional music from various regions around the world, including Brazil.

 - **The International Council for Traditional Music (ICTM)** promotes the study, practice, and appreciation of traditional music worldwide, fostering international collaboration and educational initiatives that contribute to the preservation of diverse cultural musical practices, including those from Brazil.

3. Cultural Institutions and Festivals:
 - **The WOMEX (World Music Expo)** is an annual international music conference and showcase event that features a diverse range of traditional music from different cultures worldwide, providing a platform for artists, cultural institutions, and music enthusiasts to connect, collaborate, and promote traditional musical practices, including those from Brazil.

 - **The Centre for Traditional Music and Dance (CTMD)** in the United States supports various cultural initiatives and music festivals that showcase traditional music and dance forms from different cultural communities, promoting cross-cultural understanding and appreciation, including Brazilian music and dance traditions.

4. Community Engagement and Participation:
 - **The Global Music Exchange (GME)** is an international organization that facilitates cultural exchange programs and community engagement initiatives focused on traditional music and dance, fostering global connections and collaborations among musicians and cultural practitioners, including those from Brazil.

 - **The International Council for Traditional Music (ICTM)** supports community-based cultural initiatives and music projects that promote the preservation and practice of traditional music and dance forms, fostering community engagement and participation on a global scale, including collaborative efforts with Brazilian cultural communities.

IX. The Evolution of Musical Styles in Colonial Brazil

The influence of colonial society played a pivotal role in shaping the development of regional musical styles in Brazil. The fusion of diverse cultural elements brought by European colonizers, enslaved Africans, and indigenous peoples during the colonial period laid the foundation for the emergence of unique musical genres that reflected the cultural syncretism and social dynamics of different regions. The impact of colonial society on the development of regional musical styles in Brazil can be understood through various key factors:

1. Cultural Interactions and Hybridization: The colonial period in Brazil witnessed extensive cultural interactions and hybridization between different ethnic groups, leading to the blending of European, African, and indigenous musical traditions. European musical elements, such as harmonies, instruments, and musical forms, became intertwined with the rhythmic structures, vocal styles, and percussive patterns of African and indigenous musical practices, giving rise to new and distinctive regional musical styles.

2. Religious and Ceremonial Influences: Colonial society brought diverse religious and ceremonial practices to Brazil, including

Catholicism, African spiritual beliefs, and indigenous rituals. These religious and ceremonial traditions had a profound impact on the development of regional musical styles, with music often serving as an integral component of religious ceremonies, processions, and cultural celebrations. The incorporation of sacred music, chants, and rhythmic expressions from different religious contexts contributed to the formation of unique regional musical repertoires.

3. Socioeconomic and Labor Dynamics: The colonial socioeconomic structure, characterized by the exploitation of enslaved Africans and the dominance of the plantation economy, influenced the evolution of distinct musical styles in different regions. Enslaved Africans brought with them their musical traditions, including various rhythmic patterns, dance forms, and musical instruments, which became integrated into the cultural fabric of local communities, contributing to the development of regional musical genres rooted in the experiences and struggles of the marginalized populations.

4. Geographical and Environmental Factors: The diverse geographical and environmental landscapes of different regions in Brazil also played a role in shaping regional musical styles. From the lush forests of the Amazon to the fertile plains of the Northeast and the urban centers of the Southeast, the natural environment influenced the development of musical instruments, rhythms, and lyrical themes that were reflective of the distinct cultural and geographical contexts of each region.

5. Resistance and Cultural Resilience: In the face of colonial oppression and cultural assimilation, regional musical styles often served as a form of resistance and cultural resilience, providing communities with a means to preserve their cultural identities, express their collective experiences, and assert their agency in the midst of social and political challenges. Through music, communities affirmed their cultural heritage, solidarity, and collective memory, fostering a sense of belonging and cultural pride that transcended the confines of colonial society.
The multifaceted influence of colonial society on the development of regional musical styles in Brazil underscores the complex

interplay of historical, cultural, and socio-economic factors that have shaped the country's diverse musical landscape, reflecting the resilience, creativity, and cultural vitality of its diverse communities.

X. Distinct Musical Genres from Various Regions in Brazil

Experiencing the music from this list might be the most complex and daunting undertaking for the student of Brazilian music. It provides an overview of a very diverse musical sensibility, evolved traditions and sonic experimentation. The shear inexhaustible depth represented by this most basic of overviews is why I became enraptured by the subject on visceral, emotional and intellectual levels. Let's take a look.

Northeast Region:

1. Forró: A lively genre characterized by its infectious rhythms and dance-friendly beats, originating from the northeastern states of Brazil. Forró combines elements of traditional folk music with influences from European polkas and African beats, creating a vibrant and dynamic musical style that is often associated with festive celebrations and social gatherings.

2. Frevo: Hailing from the state of Pernambuco, Frevo is a fast-paced and energetic music and dance genre that is prominently featured during the vibrant Carnival festivities in the region. Known for its lively brass instrumentation and spirited choreography, Frevo embodies the exuberance and cultural vibrancy of the Northeastern Brazilian culture.

3. Baião: A popular folk genre with roots in the northeastern state of Bahia, Baião features a distinctive rhythmic pattern and incorporates elements of indigenous and Afro-Brazilian musical traditions. Marked by its syncopated rhythms and melodious accordion melodies, Baião has become an enduring symbol of the rich cultural heritage of the Northeastern region.

Southeast Region:

1. Samba: Originating from the urban centers of Rio de Janeiro and São Paulo, Samba is a lively and rhythmic musical genre that has become synonymous with Brazilian identity worldwide. Known for its infectious beats, intricate percussion, and expressive dance movements, Samba embodies the spirit of joy, resilience, and cultural pride, serving as a cornerstone of Brazil's musical legacy.

2. Choro: Recognized as one of Brazil's earliest instrumental music styles, Choro is characterized by its intricate melodies, improvisational flair, and rich harmonies. Originating in the urban centers of Rio de Janeiro in the 19th century, Choro combines elements of European classical music with African rhythms and Brazilian folk melodies, showcasing the country's diverse cultural influences and musical innovation.

3. Bossa Nova: An influential musical movement that emerged in the 1950s and 1960s, Bossa Nova is renowned for its sophisticated harmonies, smooth melodies, and poetic lyrics. Originating in the affluent neighborhoods of Rio de Janeiro, Bossa Nova represents a fusion of Samba rhythms with elements of jazz, highlighting Brazil's capacity for musical refinement and cultural creativity.

North Region:

1. Carimbó: Rooted in the cultural traditions of the Amazon region, Carimbó is a vibrant and rhythmic dance music genre characterized by its infectious percussion, call-and-response vocals, and lively dance movements. With origins in indigenous and Afro-Brazilian musical practices, Carimbó serves as a testament to the cultural resilience and communal spirit of the Northern Brazilian communities.

2. Boi Bumba: A folkloric musical spectacle originating from the Amazonian state of Pará, Boi Bumba is a theatrical performance that combines music, dance, and storytelling. Celebrating the cultural fusion of indigenous, African, and European influences, Boi Bumba features elaborate costumes, vibrant musical ensembles, and elaborate choreography, depicting mythical tales and cultural narratives unique to the Amazonian heritage.

3. Lambada: A popular dance music genre that gained international recognition in the late 1980s, Lambada is characterized by its catchy melodies, up-tempo rhythms, and sensual dance movements. Originating in the northern state of Pará, Lambada incorporates elements of Caribbean and Latin American musical styles, creating an infectious and energetic sound that continues to captivate audiences worldwide.

South Region:

1. Gaucho Music: Reflecting the cultural traditions of the Southern state of Rio Grande do Sul, Gaucho Music embodies the spirit of the Gaucho, the South Brazilian cowboy. Marked by its heartfelt melodies, introspective lyrics, and acoustic guitar accompaniment, Gaucho Music portrays the tales of rural life, love, and nostalgia, encapsulating the cultural heritage and rugged landscapes of the Southern Brazilian plains.

2. Chamamé: Originating from the border regions of Brazil and Argentina, Chamamé is a traditional folk music genre known for its lively and expressive dance rhythms, intricate accordion melodies, and heartfelt poetic lyrics. Rooted in the cultural traditions of the South, Chamamé captures the essence of cross-cultural exchange and mutual influences between the two neighboring countries, highlighting the shared heritage and historical connections of the region.

Central-West Region:

1. Sertanejo: A popular music genre originating from the rural heartlands of Brazil, Sertanejo embodies the sentiments of rural life, love, and nature. Characterized by its heartfelt ballads, acoustic guitar accompaniment, and poetic storytelling, Sertanejo portrays the cultural traditions and rustic charm of the Central-Western Brazilian communities, paying homage to the region's agricultural heritage and pastoral landscapes.

2. Catira: A traditional folk dance and music genre that originated in the Central-Western states of Brazil, Catira features synchronized rhythmic footwork, hand-clapping, and vibrant musical accompaniment. Celebrating the communal spirit and cultural resilience of rural communities, Catira serves as a testament to the shared heritage and collective identity of the Central-Western Brazilian regions.

3. Cururu: Rooted in the cultural traditions of the Central-Western states, Cururu is a traditional folk music genre characterized by its call-and-response vocals, lively percussion, and storytelling lyrics. Often performed during religious festivals and community gatherings, Cururu embodies the spiritual devotion and cultural expressions of the Central-Western Brazilian communities, reflecting the interplay between music, faith, and communal celebration.

§

The depth and diversity represented by the list of musical genres across various regions of Brazil indeed highlight the country's rich cultural tapestry and vibrant musical heritage. Brazil's multifaceted cultural landscape is a testament to the intricate fusion of indigenous, European, and African influences, which have shaped the development of an extensive array of musical styles and traditions.

In comparison to many other cultures around the world, Brazil's musical diversity stands out for its profound intermixing of cultural elements from different continents, resulting in a unique blend of rhythms, melodies, and dance forms that reflect the country's complex historical and social dynamics. This rich amalgamation has given rise to a remarkable spectrum of musical genres, each rooted in specific regional contexts and narratives, underscoring the depth of Brazil's cultural roots and the resilience of its diverse communities.

While various cultures globally boast their own distinct musical traditions, what sets Brazil apart is the remarkable extent of hybridization and syncretism that has taken place, yielding an extraordinary breadth of musical expression that resonates with audiences worldwide. The fusion of indigenous, European, and African cultural legacies has not only contributed to the creation of diverse musical genres but has also enriched the global cultural landscape, offering a profound glimpse into the complexities of cultural exchange and the enduring power of music as a universal language of human expression.

X. Impact of Cultural Exchange on Musical Identity

The gradual synthesis of indigenous, European, and African musical elements in Brazilian music is a testament to the intricate process of cultural fusion and cross-pollination that has shaped the country's rich and diverse musical landscape over the centuries. This synthesis reflects the complex historical and social dynamics of Brazil, characterized by the colonial legacy of European conquest, the transatlantic slave trade, and the cultural resilience of indigenous communities. Several key factors have contributed to this gradual synthesis:

1. Indigenous Musical Elements:
  - Indigenous musical elements in Brazilian music are characterized by their use of natural sounds, percussive rhythms, and vocal chants that reflect a deep connection to the land, nature, and ancestral traditions. Instruments such as maracas, flutes, and drums have found their way into various Brazilian musical genres, contributing to the rhythmic complexity and earthy timbres that define the country's musical identity.

2. European Musical Influences:
  - European musical influences brought by Portuguese colonizers encompassed a wide range of classical, folk, and religious music traditions. European instruments such as the guitar, violin, and accordion were integrated into Brazilian music, influencing harmonic structures, melodic phrasing, and instrumental arrangements. These influences laid the foundation for various Brazilian genres, including choro, samba, and Bossa Nova, which

reflect a fusion of European tonalities with local rhythms and melodies.

3. African Rhythmic Expressions:
- African musical elements were introduced through the transatlantic slave trade, bringing with them a rich tapestry of rhythmic expressions, polyrhythms, and percussive traditions. Instruments such as the berimbau, atabaque, and agogô, along with intricate rhythmic patterns and call-and-response vocal styles, significantly influenced Brazilian music, particularly in genres such as samba, capoeira, and maracatu, infusing them with vibrant energy and complex rhythmic layers.

The gradual synthesis of these diverse musical elements in Brazilian music represents a continuous process of cultural negotiation, adaptation, and creative innovation, resulting in a dynamic and multifaceted musical heritage that transcends cultural boundaries and resonates with audiences worldwide. This synthesis serves as a testament to the resilience of Brazil's cultural fabric, embodying the spirit of cultural hybridity and artistic ingenuity that has defined the country's musical identity and contributed to its global cultural significance.

§

The formation of a unique Brazilian musical identity is a complex narrative that intertwines historical, cultural, and social threads, ultimately giving rise to a multifaceted musical heritage that is both deeply rooted in tradition and continuously evolving. This unique identity has been shaped by a confluence of indigenous, European, and African musical influences, reflecting Brazil's intricate history of colonization, slavery, and cultural exchange. The lasting impact of this musical identity can be observed through several key dimensions:

1. Cultural Fusion and Syncretism:
- The synthesis of diverse musical elements from indigenous, European, and African traditions has fostered a culture of artistic syncretism, resulting in a rich tapestry of rhythms, melodies, and vocal styles that epitomize the cultural diversity and vibrancy

of Brazil. This fusion has not only shaped various regional musical genres but has also permeated other aspects of Brazilian cultural expression, including dance, visual arts, and literature, reinforcing the country's position as a global cultural hub.

2. Global Recognition and Influence:

- Brazil's unique musical identity has garnered global recognition and influence, captivating audiences around the world with its infectious rhythms, expressive melodies, and vibrant performances. Genres such as samba, Bossa Nova, and Tropicália have transcended geographical boundaries, leaving an indelible mark on the global music scene and inspiring numerous artists and musicians across continents. The international success of Brazilian music has contributed to the promotion of cultural exchange, fostering a deeper appreciation of Brazil's cultural heritage and fostering cross-cultural dialogue.

3. Social Cohesion and National Pride:

- Brazilian music has played a pivotal role in fostering social cohesion and nurturing a sense of national pride among its diverse population. Music serves as a powerful medium for Brazilians to celebrate their cultural heritage, express their collective experiences, and affirm their shared identity, transcending socio-economic and regional disparities. Festivals, concerts, and musical gatherings serve as platforms for fostering unity, solidarity, and cultural resilience, reinforcing the intrinsic connection between music and the collective spirit of the Brazilian people.

4. Cultural Resilience and Representation:

- The enduring impact of Brazilian musical identity lies in its capacity to embody cultural resilience and representation, serving as a vehicle for reclaiming historical narratives, preserving ancestral traditions, and advocating for social justice and cultural preservation. Through music, marginalized communities have found a voice to articulate their struggles, aspirations, and cultural legacies, empowering them to assert their place within the broader cultural landscape and advocate for greater social inclusion and cultural recognition.

The formation of a unique Brazilian musical identity continues to transcend temporal and spatial boundaries, resonating with audiences across generations and cultures, and serving as a testament to the enduring power of music as a catalyst for cultural expression, social transformation, and global interconnectedness.

Chapter 2: The Emergence of Popular Brazilian Music: Exploring the Choro Tradition and the Influence of European Classical Music

Choro

Choro, known as the "soul" of Brazilian music, stands as a foundational genre that embodies the rich cultural heritage and musical ingenuity of Brazil. With its origins tracing back to the vibrant streets and intimate gatherings of 19th-century Rio de Janeiro, Choro has flourished as a quintessential expression of Brazilian musical identity. This enchanting musical style, characterized by its intricate melodies, lively rhythms, and improvisational virtuosity, encapsulates the spirit of Brazilian cultural fusion, blending European influences with indigenous and African rhythms to create a unique and enchanting musical experience. As a testament to the country's enduring musical legacy, Choro has not only shaped the trajectory of Brazilian popular music but has also served as a vital cultural bridge, uniting diverse communities and fostering a sense of shared musical heritage. With its infectious energy, heartfelt melodies, and rich historical significance, Choro continues to resonate with audiences worldwide, inviting them on a captivating journey through the heart and soul of Brazil's musical narrative.

Choro, with its rich historical legacy and dynamic musical elements, has played a pivotal role in bridging cultural divides and fostering a profound sense of musical cross-pollination within Brazilian society. As a genre that embodies a fusion of diverse cultural influences, Choro serves as a cultural ambassador, transcending geographical, social, and ethnic boundaries to create a harmonious convergence of musical traditions. By seamlessly integrating elements of European classical music, African rhythms, and indigenous melodies, Choro has facilitated a cultural dialogue that transcends historical divisions, forging a shared musical language that resonates with people from all walks of life. Its lively and expressive compositions have served as a meeting point for musicians from various cultural backgrounds, encouraging collaborative exchange and artistic innovation. Through its infectious rhythms and melodic intricacies, Choro has not only united communities but has also fostered a deep appreciation for cultural diversity and artistic expression, emphasizing the power of music as a universal language that transcends cultural differences and fosters mutual understanding and respect.

European Classical Music

The influence of European classical music on the formation of Brazilian musical styles has left an indelible mark on the country's cultural landscape, shaping the evolution of diverse genres and contributing to the rich tapestry of Brazil's musical identity. With the arrival of Portuguese colonizers and the establishment of colonial society, European musical traditions permeated Brazilian cultural expressions, laying the groundwork for a transformative musical dialogue. Elements of European classical music, including symphonic compositions, harmonic structures, and formal arrangements, found resonance in Brazil's musical fabric, gradually intertwining with indigenous and African musical elements to give rise to unique and innovative styles. This transformative exchange between European classical music and local musical sensibilities not only enriched the sonic palette of Brazilian music but also facilitated the emergence of new hybrid genres, reflecting the dynamic interplay between cultural traditions and artistic innovation. As a result, the impact of European classical music serves as a crucial touchstone in understanding the intricate layers of Brazil's musical heritage, underscoring the country's profound capacity for cultural synthesis and creative reinvention.

I. The Rise of Choro Tradition

Choro is a predominantly instrumental music tradition that emerged in Brazil around 1870. It is considered the father of samba and the grandfather of Bossa Nova. The following is a historical overview of the origins and evolution of the Choro tradition from the 19th century to the present day:

- **19th Century:** The tradition of musicians earning their living as barbers traces its roots to Italy and was exported to Brazil. Choro began as a way of interpreting European dance music, such as the polka and the waltz, with African rhythms and improvisation. The word "choro" was first used to designate a genre in 1889 with the publication of Chiquinha Gonzaga's composition "Só no choro" (Only in Choro) .

- **Early 20th Century:** Choro became a popular urban music style in Brazil, with composers such as Ernesto Nazareth and Pixinguinha contributing to its development. Choro was also associated with Brazilian nationalism and was seen as a way to assert Brazil's cultural identity.

- **Mid-20th Century:** Choro declined in popularity as other music styles, such as samba and Bossa Nova, gained prominence. Choro musicians had historically been amateurs, earning their living by other means, and eschewing internal competition and modernization to keep choro the musical, almost spiritual, expression of their community.

- **Late 20th Century:** The decade of the 1970s revitalized choro, increased choro repertoire and recordings, educated a new generation of performers, and solidified choro's historical importance. However, in the process, it changed choro's social context forever. Choro moved into the 21st century and began to reach a larger international audience.

- **Present Day:** Choro is transcending its original community and is becoming more international. The key to maintaining choro's cultural integrity during the process of internationalization is to keep its performance practice a vital part of the music. Choro musicians continue the work of generations of musicians and composers who created and developed the style before them.

Choro is a rich and complex musical tradition that has evolved over the past century and a half. It has been influenced by European dance music, African rhythms, and Brazilian nationalism. Choro has experienced periods of popularity and decline, but it has remained an important part of Brazil's cultural heritage.

Today, Choro is reaching a larger international audience, and it is important to maintain its cultural integrity during the process of internationalization.

II. Musical Characteristics of Churo

The following is a detailed exploration of the distinctive musical characteristics that define Choro music:

1. Instrumental Arrangements:
Choro is characterized by its distinctive instrumental arrangements, typically featuring a small ensemble of musicians, including instruments such as the flute, guitar, cavaquinho, and bandolim (Brazilian mandolin). These instruments work in tandem to create a rich and layered sonic texture, allowing for intricate melodic interplay and rhythmic complexity that define the genre.

2. Harmonic Structures:
Choro often employs sophisticated harmonic structures, blending elements of European classical music with syncopated rhythms and jazz-inspired chord progressions. The harmonic language of Choro is marked by its use of extended chords, chromaticism, and modulations, creating a harmonic depth that is both expressive and technically intricate.

3. Rhythmic Variations:
The rhythmic patterns in Choro are characterized by their lively and syncopated nature, often featuring complex polyrhythms and cross-rhythmic interactions between different instrumental voices. The interplay of duple and triple meter rhythms, coupled

with the use of intricate syncopation, contributes to the energetic and dynamic pulse that defines Choro music.

4. Melodic Ornamentation:
Choro is renowned for its melodic ornamentation, incorporating elaborate flourishes, trills, and rapid scalar passages that showcase the virtuosic abilities of the performers. The use of melodic embellishments, such as glissandos, grace notes, and appoggiaturas, adds a sense of expressiveness and improvisational flair to the musical phrases, allowing for nuanced and emotive interpretations of the compositions.

5. Improvisational Techniques:
A hallmark of Choro music is its emphasis on improvisation, allowing musicians to engage in spontaneous musical dialogue and creative exploration during performances. Improvisational techniques in Choro often involve melodic variations, call-and-response interactions, and collaborative improvisation among ensemble members, fostering a sense of musical camaraderie and expressive freedom within the performance context.

The intricate interplay of these musical characteristics distinguishes Choro as a genre that embodies both technical sophistication and emotive depth, showcasing the musical virtuosity and creative spirit of its performers while honoring the genre's rich historical legacy and cultural significance.

§

Choro holds significant social and cultural importance as a form of artistic expression and a communal identity in Brazilian society. Its enduring presence has contributed to the preservation of cultural heritage, the cultivation of musical traditions, and the fostering of a sense of collective identity among diverse communities. Several key points contribute to its social and cultural significance:

1. Cultural Heritage Preservation: Choro serves as a vessel for preserving Brazil's rich cultural heritage, reflecting the country's diverse musical history and the interplay of various cultural influences. By maintaining traditional instrumentation, harmonic structures, and improvisational techniques, Choro acts as a cultural repository, safeguarding the musical legacy of past generations and passing it down to future ones.

2. Community Cohesion: Choro has played a crucial role in fostering community cohesion and social interaction, providing a platform for people from different backgrounds to come together, share experiences, and celebrate their shared cultural heritage. Its presence in intimate gatherings, local venues, and cultural events has facilitated the formation of close-knit musical communities, nurturing a sense of belonging and solidarity among musicians and enthusiasts alike.

3. Artistic Innovation and Creativity: Choro encourages artistic innovation and creativity, allowing musicians to reinterpret traditional compositions, experiment with improvisational techniques, and explore new musical possibilities. This creative freedom has not only propelled the evolution of Choro but has also inspired the development of new musical styles, contributing to the dynamic and ever-evolving landscape of Brazilian popular music.

4. Cultural Identity and National Pride: Choro embodies a sense of cultural identity and national pride, serving as a symbol of Brazilian musical excellence and artistic prowess. Its intricate melodies, rhythmic intricacies, and expressive nuances reflect the spirit of Brazilian creativity and innovation, instilling a sense of pride and admiration for the country's cultural contributions to the global music scene.

5. Educational and Pedagogical Significance: Choro plays a vital role in music education and pedagogy, serving as a foundational genre for aspiring musicians to learn essential techniques, explore improvisational skills, and develop a deep understanding of Brazilian musical traditions. Its educational significance extends to the transmission of cultural values, musical techniques, and historical narratives, ensuring the continuity of Choro's legacy for future generations.

By embodying these social and cultural dimensions, Choro has emerged as more than just a musical genre; it has become a cultural phenomenon that embodies the spirit of artistic expression, communal engagement, and national pride, contributing to the enrichment of Brazil's cultural heritage and global artistic legacy.

Suggested Listening

1. "Brasileirinho" (1970) by Waldir Azevedo
- Label: Continental
- Release Date: 1970
- Description: This iconic recording by Waldir Azevedo epitomizes the essence of traditional Choro music, featuring the characteristic sounds of the cavaquinho and showcasing Azevedo's virtuosity. Its inclusion represents a timeless classic within the Choro repertoire.

2. "Choros do Brasil" (2016) by Trio Madeira Brasil
- Label: Acari Records
- Release Date: 2016
- Description: Trio Madeira Brasil's "Choros do Brasil" offers a contemporary perspective on Choro, infusing traditional elements with modern interpretations, showcasing the genre's continued relevance and adaptability within the contemporary Brazilian music scene.

3. "Tico-Tico no Fubá" (1950) by Zequinha de Abreu
- Label: Odeon
- Release Date: 1950
- Description: Zequinha de Abreu's "Tico-Tico no Fubá" represents a quintessential Choro composition that has achieved widespread international recognition, highlighting the genre's ability to transcend cultural boundaries and captivate global audiences with its infectious melodies and lively rhythms.

4. "Choro de Bolso" (2019) by Regional Tira-Teima
  - Label: Independently released
  - Release Date: 2019
  - Description: "Choro de Bolso" by Regional Tira-Teima exemplifies the contemporary vitality of Choro music, featuring a dynamic ensemble that skillfully preserves the traditional Choro style while incorporating innovative arrangements and improvisational techniques, showcasing the genre's enduring appeal among modern musicians and audiences.

5. "Carinhoso" (1936) by Pixinguinha
  - Label: Odeon
  - Release Date: 1936
  - Description: Pixinguinha's "Carinhoso" stands as a timeless masterpiece within the Choro repertoire, renowned for its lyrical beauty and emotional depth, symbolizing the genre's capacity to evoke a profound sense of nostalgia, romance, and cultural pride through its melodic expressiveness and harmonic richness.

6. "Doce de Coco" (1962) by Jacob do Bandolim
  - Label: Continental
  - Release Date: 1962
  - Description: Jacob do Bandolim's "Doce de Coco" exemplifies the virtuosity and technical brilliance of Choro music, showcasing the intricate interplay of melodic and rhythmic elements, and underscoring the genre's capacity for dynamic and expressive musical storytelling.

7. "Choro Livre" (2017) by Quarteto Moderno
  - Label: Biscoito Fino
  - Release Date: 2017
  - Description: Quarteto Moderno's "Choro Livre" represents a contemporary exploration of Choro's melodic intricacies and improvisational agility, showcasing the ensemble's collective virtuosity and creative synergy, and demonstrating the genre's adaptability to modern musical sensibilities.

8. "Lamentos" (1976) by Altamiro Carrilho
  - Label: RCA Victor

- Release Date: 1976
- Description: Altamiro Carrilho's "Lamentos" serves as a testament to the emotional depth and expressive range of Choro music, conveying a sense of melancholy and introspection through its poignant melodies and nuanced musical phrasing, thus highlighting the genre's capacity for evocative storytelling and emotional resonance.

9. "Noites Cariocas" (1977) by Jacob do Bandolim
- Label: EMI-Odeon
- Release Date: 1977
- Description: Jacob do Bandolim's "Noites Cariocas" captures the vibrant and lively spirit of Choro music, featuring dynamic rhythmic patterns, spirited melodic motifs, and intricate improvisational dialogues, reflecting the genre's capacity for playful musical exchanges and joyful communal celebration.

10. "Rosa" (1957) by Pixinguinha
- Label: Continental
- Release Date: 1957
- Description: Pixinguinha's "Rosa" exemplifies the timeless elegance and poetic beauty of Choro music, showcasing the genre's capacity for lyrical storytelling and melodic sophistication, and highlighting its enduring appeal as a source of cultural inspiration and artistic expression.

These selected Choro compositions and recordings offer a diverse and comprehensive listening experience, showcasing the virtuosity, diversity, and historical significance of the Choro tradition in Brazilian music.

III. Influence of European Classic Compositions on Brazilian Composers

The influence of European classical music on early Brazilian popular music is a rich and complex topic that highlights the cultural exchange between Europe and Brazil during the colonial and post-colonial periods. This influence can be seen in various aspects of Brazilian music, including its melodies, harmonies, instrumentation, and overall musical structure. Here are some key points to consider:

1. Colonial Influences: During the colonial period, Portugal had a significant influence on Brazilian culture, including its music. European classical music, particularly the Baroque and Classical styles, was brought to Brazil by Portuguese colonizers. This laid the foundation for the integration of European musical elements into the emerging Brazilian music scene.

2. Choral Music and Church Influence: European choral music, including liturgical compositions and hymns, greatly influenced early Brazilian music. The use of choral arrangements and polyphonic structures in religious music had an impact on the development of vocal music in Brazil.

3. Opera and Theatrical Music: The introduction of opera and theatrical music in Brazil also brought European classical elements to the forefront. Brazilian composers and musicians were exposed to European operatic styles, leading to the incorporation of operatic techniques and dramatic expressions in Brazilian popular music.

4. Dance Forms and Rhythms: European dances such as the minuet, waltz, and polka were incorporated into Brazilian popular music, leading to the creation of new hybrid genres. These European dance forms were often blended with African and indigenous rhythms, resulting in unique Brazilian musical styles.

5. Influence on Instrumentation: The use of European classical instruments, such as violins, cellos, and flutes, was integrated into early Brazilian popular music. These instruments were often combined with traditional Brazilian instruments like the cavaquinho and the berimbau, leading to the development of distinctive Brazilian musical ensembles.

6. Musical Education and Academia: The establishment of music schools and conservatories in Brazil, following European models, played a crucial role in disseminating European classical music knowledge. This led to the training of Brazilian musicians in European classical techniques and forms, which subsequently influenced their compositions and performances in the realm of Brazilian popular music.

7. Cultural Synthesis and Transformation: Over time, Brazilian musicians creatively transformed and adapted European classical elements to reflect their own cultural identity and musical sensibilities. This process of cultural synthesis gave rise to unique Brazilian musical genres, such as choro, samba, and Bossa Nova, which incorporated elements of European classical music while retaining distinct Brazilian characteristics.

The influence of European classical music on early Brazilian popular music was instrumental in shaping the rich and diverse musical heritage of Brazil. This cultural exchange not only enriched the Brazilian music scene but also contributed to the global recognition of Brazilian music as a vibrant and dynamic cultural phenomenon.

Suggested Listening

Certainly, here are the suggested European compositions with detailed explanations highlighting their significance and relevance to the influence of European classical music on early Brazilian popular music:

1. Giuseppe Verdi - "Aida" (1871, Decca Records): Verdi's grand opera "Aida" serves as a prime example of the dramatic and powerful musical style that greatly influenced Brazilian operatic compositions. Its intricate orchestration and emotionally charged arias left a lasting impact on Brazilian composers, influencing the development of their own operatic works.

2. Johann Strauss II - "Blue Danube Waltz" (1867, Sony Classical): Strauss's famous waltz represents the elegance and vivacity of European dance music that found its way into the fabric of Brazilian popular music. The graceful melodies and rhythmic charm of this waltz style influenced Brazilian composers, inspiring them to infuse their own traditional rhythms and melodies with European dance elements.

3. Joaquín Rodrigo - "Concierto de Aranjuez" (1940, Deutsche Grammophon): Rodrigo's renowned guitar concerto embodies the essence of Spanish musical heritage, which shares commonalities with the rich musical tapestry of Brazil. The fusion of Spanish and European classical elements in Rodrigo's work demonstrates the potential for cross-cultural synthesis, an approach that inspired Brazilian composers seeking to integrate their own cultural heritage into their compositions.

4. Claude Debussy - "Clair de Lune" (1905, Naxos): Debussy's impressionistic masterpiece "Clair de Lune" illustrates the subtle nuances and evocative qualities that influenced Brazilian composers in their exploration of mood and atmosphere within their own musical creations. Its delicate yet profound tonal palette resonated with Brazilian musicians, encouraging them to experiment with similar emotional depth and expressiveness in their compositions.

By examining these influential European compositions, we can understand the diverse range of musical styles and techniques that inspired Brazilian composers to integrate European classical elements into their own works, resulting in a unique fusion that defined early Brazilian popular music. Now to the Brazilian compositions.

1. Heitor Villa-Lobos - "Yerma" (1958, EMI Classics): Villa-Lobos's operatic work "Yerma" exemplifies the fusion of Brazilian folk elements with the dramatic and structural influences of European operatic styles. Through this synthesis, Villa-Lobos effectively integrated Brazilian themes and rhythms with the grandeur and emotional depth characteristic of European classical operas.
2. Ernesto Nazareth - "Odeon" (1910, Biscoito Fino): Nazareth's

composition "Odeon" represents the amalgamation of European dance forms, particularly the waltz, with the lively and syncopated rhythms of Brazilian choro music. This fusion highlights the influence of European dance traditions on the development of Brazilian popular music, showcasing the adaptability and creativity of Brazilian composers.

3. Radamés Gnattali - "Concerto for Guitar and Orchestra" (1956, BIS): Gnattali's concerto exemplifies the integration of European classical traditions with Brazilian musical elements, as demonstrated through the skillful orchestration and incorporation of the guitar. This blending of European orchestral techniques with Brazilian musical sensibilities reflects the dynamic cultural exchange that shaped early Brazilian classical compositions.

4. Antônio Carlos Jobim - "Desafinado" (1959, Verve Records): Jobim's "Desafinado" combines the harmonies of jazz with the rhythmic foundations of Brazilian samba, showcasing the influence of European jazz and impressionist elements on the development of Bossa Nova. Through this fusion, Jobim successfully introduced a sophisticated and nuanced approach to Brazilian popular music, intertwining European and Brazilian musical sensibilities.

5. Heitor Villa-Lobos - "Bachianas Brasileiras No. 5" (1945, Sony Classical): Villa-Lobos's "Bachianas Brasileiras No. 5" demonstrates the harmonious blend of Brazilian and European classical music, featuring a combination of operatic vocal lines with the rich textures of the cello ensemble. This fusion highlights the composer's efforts to integrate Brazilian melodies and rhythms with the structural and harmonic elements of European classical compositions.

6. Heitor Villa-Lobos - "Trenzinho Caipira" (1930, RCA Red Seal): "Trenzinho Caipira" reflects Villa-Lobos's incorporation of Brazilian folk melodies with Western classical elements. This piece, inspired by the rhythmic patterns of a rural train journey, showcases the composer's ability to infuse European classical techniques with distinctly Brazilian musical themes, thus establishing a unique and evocative musical narrative.

7. Waldir Azevedo - "Brasileirinho" (1947, EMI Brasil): Azevedo's "Brasileirinho" exemplifies the integration of European waltz influences with the lively and intricate rhythms of Brazilian choro music. This fusion highlights the cross-cultural exchange between European and Brazilian musical traditions, showcasing Azevedo's creative adaptation of European dance elements within the context of Brazilian popular music.

§

Understanding the connections between European music and Brazilian music involves a multifaceted approach, depending on your level of expertise and interest.

Whether you are a novice listener, a musician, or an academic, here are some specific points to consider:

1. Novice Listeners:
 - Listen for familiar musical elements such as melodies, harmonies, and rhythms that resemble those found in European classical music. Note how these elements are integrated into the Brazilian compositions, creating a unique fusion of styles.

 - Pay attention to the emotional impact and the overall mood conveyed by the music. Compare the feelings evoked by both European and Brazilian compositions, noticing any similarities or differences in the expression of themes and emotions.

2. Musicians:
 - Analyze the musical structures and techniques used in both European and Brazilian compositions. Look for common compositional approaches, such as the use of specific chord progressions, thematic development, and orchestration techniques that demonstrate the influence of European classical music on Brazilian compositions.

- Focus on the instrumentation and arrangement, noting how Brazilian composers incorporate European classical instruments into traditional Brazilian ensembles. Identify the ways in which these instruments interact and blend to create a distinctive sound that combines European and Brazilian musical elements.

3. Academics:
- Conduct comparative analyses of specific musical elements, including harmonic progressions, melodic patterns, and rhythmic variations in European and Brazilian compositions. Document how these elements have been adapted and transformed to reflect the unique cultural context of Brazil.

- Explore the historical and socio-cultural influences that facilitated the exchange between European and Brazilian musical traditions. Investigate the impact of colonization, migration, and cultural integration on the evolution of Brazilian music, highlighting key moments of cross-cultural exchange and musical dialogue.

4. Cultural Historians:
- Examine the socio-political and historical context surrounding the development of European classical music and its subsequent influence on early Brazilian popular music. Consider the impact of colonialism, cultural exchange, and the emergence of a distinct Brazilian musical identity.

- Trace the evolution of Brazilian musical genres, identifying specific instances where European classical elements have been adapted and transformed to accommodate the unique cultural expressions and traditions of Brazil. Analyze how these transformations have shaped the cultural narrative and identity of Brazilian music over time.

By approaching the study of European and Brazilian music with these specific perspectives, you can gain a comprehensive understanding of the connections and influences that have shaped the rich and diverse musical heritage of Brazil.

Chapter 3. Rhythms of Resilience: The Golden Era of Samba in Brazil

In the sultry nights of Rio de Janeiro, amidst the pulsating energy of bustling streets and the rhythmic sway of bodies in motion, a cultural phenomenon was born. The golden era of samba in Brazil stands as a testament to the indomitable spirit of a people, as their music echoed the resilience, hope, and cultural richness of a nation in transition. This chapter embarks on a captivating journey through the colorful history and multifaceted tapestry of samba, delving into the socio-cultural intricacies that shaped its emergence and solidified its place as the soulful heartbeat of Brazilian identity.

With roots deeply embedded in the vibrant communities of Brazil, samba emerged as a potent form of artistic expression, transcending its origins as a local musical tradition to become a symbol of unity and empowerment for the masses. From the smoky bars of the favelas to the grand stages of international acclaim, samba captivated the hearts and minds of a diverse populace, fostering a sense of belonging and pride in a country undergoing profound social and political changes.

Within these pages, we unravel the narratives of legendary musicians, unsung heroes, and passionate advocates whose contributions propelled samba into the global spotlight. We uncover the echoes of African rhythms, European harmonies, and indigenous melodies that harmoniously converged to create the vibrant soundscape of samba, a testament to the cultural synthesis and resilience that defined Brazil's rich musical heritage.

As we navigate the cultural crossroads of the golden era, we examine the profound impact of samba on the socio-political fabric of Brazilian society, revealing its role as a catalyst for social change, cultural preservation, and the assertion of identity. Through this exploration, we aim to illuminate the enduring legacy of samba and its enduring significance as an emblem of

Brazil's cultural vibrancy and enduring spirit of resilience. Step into the world of samba and immerse yourself in the enchanting melodies, poignant lyrics, and spirited rhythms that continue to resonate across the landscapes of Brazil and beyond.

Initial Listening Suggestions

For a music student new to samba, here are some immediate listening suggestions that progress from early recordings to the Golden Age, including brief biographies of the main artists and notable musicians playing on the albums:

1. "Pelo Telefone" (1917) - Donga:
This is considered the first recorded samba. Donga, known as Ernesto dos Santos, was a key figure in the early development of samba in Rio de Janeiro. The song was recorded by Banda Odeon.

2. "Na Baixa do Sapateiro" (1939) - Carmen Miranda:
Carmen Miranda was a Brazilian samba singer and actress known for popularizing Brazilian music internationally. Her recording of "Na Baixa do Sapateiro," also known as "Bahia," captures the vibrant spirit of Brazilian samba and showcases her dynamic vocal style. Recorded under the label Odeon Records.

3. "Chega de Saudade" (1959) - João Gilberto:
João Gilberto, a renowned Brazilian guitarist and singer, is often referred to as the father of Bossa Nova. His recording of "Chega de Saudade" marks the beginning of the Bossa Nova movement, a genre closely related to samba. Released under Odeon Records.

4. "A Voz do Morro" (1955) - Elizeth Cardoso:
Elizeth Cardoso, known as "A Divina," was a prominent Brazilian samba and Bossa Nova singer. Her album "A Voz do Morro" exemplifies the emotional depth and expressive power of her voice, highlighting her influential role in the Golden Age of samba. Released under the label Copacabana.

5. "Carnaval da Velha Guarda" (1965) - Various Artists:
This album features a compilation of samba tracks by renowned samba musicians from the Golden Age, including Cartola, Nelson Cavaquinho, and Clementina de Jesus. It showcases the diverse styles and influences that defined the pinnacle of samba's cultural significance. Released under the label RCA Victor.

By listening to these recordings, the student can trace the evolution of samba from its early roots to its peak during the Golden Age, gaining a comprehensive understanding of the genre's historical and cultural significance.

§

Focus: Carmen Miranda

Carmen Miranda (1909-1955), born Maria do Carmo Miranda da Cunha, was a Portuguese-born Brazilian samba singer, dancer, and actress. Known for her vivacious personality, colorful costumes, and distinctive headpieces adorned with fruit, she became an iconic figure in the entertainment industry during the mid-20th century. Miranda rose to fame in Brazil before gaining international recognition in the United States, where she became a symbol of Latin American culture and musical exuberance.

Recording and Film Importance

Miranda's recordings, such as "Tico-Tico no Fubá" and "O Que É Que a Baiana Tem," showcased her energetic vocal style and her ability to infuse samba rhythms with a unique blend of Brazilian and Latin American musical elements. Her recordings contributed to the popularization of Brazilian music internationally, serving as an introduction to the vibrant sounds of samba and the cultural richness of Brazil for audiences around the world.

In film, Carmen Miranda's exuberant performances in Hollywood movies, including "The Gang's All Here" (1943) and "That Night in Rio" (1941), solidified her image as the "Brazilian Bombshell" and a leading proponent of Latin American culture in mainstream

American entertainment. Her dynamic on-screen persona and infectious musical numbers helped pave the way for the global recognition of Latin American music and dance, particularly during the Golden Age of Hollywood.

Cultural Importance

Miranda's cultural importance transcends her contributions to the world of music and film. As one of the first Latin American entertainers to achieve widespread fame on the international stage, she played a vital role in popularizing Brazilian music and dance forms, including samba, across various cultural and linguistic barriers. Her spirited performances and colorful costumes helped to challenge stereotypes and promote a positive image of Latin American culture, fostering a greater appreciation for the diversity and vibrancy of the region's artistic heritage.

Legacy

Carmen Miranda's legacy endures as a symbol of Latin American cultural identity and musical dynamism. Her influence on popular culture can be seen in the continued celebration of her unique style and persona, which has inspired numerous tributes, fashion trends, and artistic homages over the years. Her impact on the global dissemination of Brazilian music and the popularization of samba remains a testament to her enduring legacy as a pioneering figure in the history of Latin American entertainment and cultural diplomacy.

I. Birth and Evolution of Samba

The birth and evolution of samba trace back to the rich cultural amalgamation in Brazil, encompassing a vibrant tapestry of African, European, and indigenous musical traditions. Originating in the vibrant neighborhoods of Rio de Janeiro, samba embodies the rhythmic pulse and cultural vibrancy that have defined Brazilian identity for centuries.

Here is a comprehensive overview of the birth and evolution of samba:

1. African Roots: Samba finds its roots in the rhythmic and percussive musical traditions brought to Brazil by African slaves during the colonial era. These traditions, deeply rooted in West African musical cultures, provided the foundation for the syncopated rhythms, call-and-response patterns, and lively percussion that characterize early forms of samba.

2. Cultural Fusion: The fusion of African musical traditions with European melodies, harmonies, and instruments, particularly during the 19th century, led to the emergence of various musical styles in Brazil. This fusion resulted in the development of distinct regional styles, including the urban samba of Rio de Janeiro, which incorporated elements of Portuguese and European musical influences.

3. Carnival and Social Movements: Samba became intertwined with the annual Carnival celebrations, providing a platform for marginalized communities to express their cultural identity, social struggles, and collective resilience. The rhythmic and spirited nature of samba provided a means for the Afro-Brazilian population to celebrate their heritage, assert their presence, and protest social injustices.

4. Recording Industry and Global Recognition: The early 20th century witnessed the rise of the recording industry, allowing samba to reach a broader audience both within Brazil and internationally. Artists such as Pixinguinha, Donga, and Ismael Silva contributed to the popularization of samba through their recordings, leading to its recognition as a significant genre in Brazilian popular music.

5. The Golden Age: The 1930s to 1950s marked the Golden Age of samba, characterized by its widespread popularity and cultural significance. Influential artists like Cartola, Ary Barroso, and Noel Rosa contributed to the diversification of samba styles, incorporating elements of jazz, blues, and traditional Brazilian melodies, thus solidifying samba's position as a cultural emblem and a reflection of Brazilian national identity.

6. Bossa Nova Influence: The late 1950s and early 1960s saw the emergence of Bossa Nova, a derivative of samba that emphasized a more subdued and refined musical style. Artists such as João Gilberto and Antônio Carlos Jobim played pivotal roles in the evolution of Brazilian music, fusing elements of samba with jazz to create a sophisticated and globally influential musical genre.

7. Modern Resurgence and Global Reach: In contemporary times, samba has experienced a resurgence, with modern artists and groups infusing traditional samba with contemporary musical elements. This has led to the global recognition of samba as a vibrant and dynamic musical genre that continues to captivate audiences worldwide, showcasing the enduring legacy and cultural significance of this quintessentially Brazilian musical tradition.

Through its profound historical roots and cultural resonance, samba stands as a testament to the resilience, creativity, and diversity of the Brazilian people, embodying the spirit of unity, celebration, and collective identity that transcends geographical boundaries and cultural barriers.

§

During the Golden Age of samba, spanning the 1930s to the 1950s, a constellation of remarkable musicians, composers, producers, and record labels contributed to the genre's cultural zenith, solidifying its position as a national emblem of Brazil. Some key figures and their contributions during this pivotal era include:

1. Pixinguinha (1897-1973): A prominent composer, arranger, and instrumentalist, Pixinguinha was instrumental in popularizing samba and choro music. His innovative compositions, such as "Carinhoso" and "Rosa," exemplify his profound influence on the development of Brazilian popular music during the Golden Age.

2. Ary Barroso (1903-1964): Known for his vibrant compositions, Ary Barroso was a prolific songwriter and one of the most influential figures in Brazilian music. His iconic piece "Aquarela do Brasil" ("Brazil") achieved international acclaim and solidified his legacy as a pioneer of samba and Brazilian popular music.

3. Noel Rosa (1910-1937): Noel Rosa, renowned for his poignant lyrics and melodious compositions, played a significant role in shaping the lyrical and thematic content of samba during the Golden Age. His works, including "Feitiço da Vila" and "Com que Roupa," remain timeless classics in the Brazilian musical canon.

4. Ismael Silva (1905-1978): A celebrated samba composer and founding member of the influential group "Os Oito Batutas," Ismael Silva was instrumental in revolutionizing the structure and style of samba compositions. His contributions to the development of samba-enredo, a style of samba performed during Carnival parades, were pivotal in shaping the genre's evolution.
5. Casa Edison: Established in 1902, Casa Edison was the first record label in Brazil, playing a crucial role in the popularization and commercialization of samba music during the early 20th century. It was responsible for recording and distributing the works of many influential samba musicians, contributing to the genre's widespread recognition.

6. RCA Victor: As a prominent record label, RCA Victor played a significant role in promoting samba music and showcasing the works of renowned samba artists during the Golden Age. Its extensive distribution network and marketing strategies contributed to the global dissemination of samba, solidifying its position as a significant cultural export from Brazil.

7. Cartola (1908-1980): Angenor de Oliveira, popularly known as Cartola, was a revered samba composer, singer, and instrumentalist. His introspective and emotive compositions, such as "As Rosas Não Falam" and "O Mundo É um Moinho," epitomize the lyrical depth and musical richness that defined the Golden Age of samba.

8. Clementina de Jesus (1901-1987): Recognized as one of the most influential samba and folk artists of her time, Clementina de Jesus revitalized traditional samba and Afro-Brazilian musical styles during the Golden Age. Her powerful and soulful renditions of samba and other traditional genres contributed to the preservation and popularization of Brazil's musical heritage.

These pioneering musicians, along with the influential record labels such as Casa Edison and RCA Victor, collectively shaped the cultural landscape of the Golden Age, leaving an indelible mark on the history and legacy of samba in Brazil.

§

Focus: RCA Victor Records

RCA Victor Records holds a storied history in the recording industry, playing a pivotal role in the popularization and dissemination of music across the globe. Founded in 1901 as the Victor Talking Machine Company, the label underwent several transformations before eventually merging with Radio Corporation of America (RCA) in 1929. With a rich legacy in the development of recording technologies and commercial distribution, RCA Victor Records became renowned for its diverse catalog, including a significant focus on samba and Brazilian recordings.

Samba and Brazilian Recordings

RCA Victor Records played a crucial role in introducing samba and Brazilian music to international audiences, capturing the rich and vibrant sounds of Brazil's musical landscape. By collaborating with prominent Brazilian artists and producers, the label facilitated the recording and distribution of influential samba compositions, contributing to the global recognition and appreciation of Brazil's rich musical heritage.

Major Artists and Figures

- Carmen Miranda: A notable artist under RCA Victor, Carmen Miranda's lively performances and recordings helped popularize Brazilian music and culture on an international scale, showcasing the label's commitment to promoting diverse musical genres and styles.

- Banda Odeon: Known for their contributions to the early samba recordings, Banda Odeon collaborated with RCA Victor, enabling the label to capture the authentic spirit and rhythms of samba music during its formative years.

- Pixinguinha: The renowned Brazilian composer and musician Pixinguinha collaborated with RCA Victor, contributing to the label's rich catalog of samba and Brazilian recordings, thereby solidifying his own legacy as a pioneering figure in the development of Brazilian popular music.

Musical, Business, and Cultural Legacy

RCA Victor Records' commitment to musical diversity and innovation left an indelible mark on the global recording industry. By fostering collaborations with diverse artists and embracing a wide range of musical genres, including samba and Brazilian music, the label contributed to the cross-cultural exchange and appreciation of world music.

From a business standpoint, RCA Victor Records' pioneering efforts in recording technologies and commercial distribution set a precedent for the modern music industry, shaping the trajectory of music production and consumption in the 20th century.

Culturally, RCA Victor Records' dedication to promoting diverse musical traditions helped foster a deeper understanding and appreciation of Brazil's rich cultural heritage, highlighting the country's vibrant musical landscape and contributing to the global recognition of samba as a significant cultural export. Through its collaborations with prominent Brazilian artists and its diverse catalog of samba recordings, RCA Victor Records cemented its legacy as a trailblazing label that played a key role in bringing the sounds of Brazil to audiences around the world.

§

Instruments Used in Samba

Samba, deeply rooted in African and Brazilian musical traditions, utilizes a diverse array of instruments that contribute to its vibrant and rhythmic sound. These instruments are crucial in creating the infectious beats and energetic melodies that characterize the genre.

Some of the key instruments used in samba include:

1. Surdo: A large bass drum that forms the foundation of the samba rhythm, providing a deep and resonant pulse that drives the music forward.

2. Tamborim: A small, handheld drum played with a stick or the fingers, adding intricate and fast-paced rhythms that embellish the samba groove.

3. Pandeiro: A type of tambourine with a head of synthetic or animal skin, producing a rich blend of jingling and percussive sounds that enhance the rhythmic complexity of the music.

4. Cavaquinho: A small string instrument resembling a ukulele, known for its bright and lively sound, often used to provide melodic and harmonic accompaniment in samba ensembles.

5. Agogô: A double bell with a high-pitched and bright tone, typically played with a stick, adding a distinctive and lively metallic timbre to the rhythmic layers of samba.

6. Cuíca: A friction drum with a unique and distinctive sound produced by rubbing a stick attached to the drumhead, creating a vocal-like effect that contributes to the expressive and dynamic nature of samba music.

Venues for Samba Performances

Samba is closely associated with vibrant cultural gatherings, lively celebrations, and community-based events, often taking place in various traditional and contemporary venues.

Some of the typical venues where samba is performed include:

1. Carnival Parades: Samba is an integral part of the elaborate and colorful Carnival parades held in cities such as Rio de Janeiro and São Paulo, where samba schools compete in a dazzling display of music, dance, and costume.

2. Samba Schools: Dedicated samba schools serve as hubs for samba rehearsals, performances, and cultural activities, fostering a sense of community and artistic expression among members and enthusiasts of the genre.

3. Street Parties and Festivals: Samba can often be heard and experienced at lively street parties and cultural festivals across Brazil, where musicians and dancers come together to celebrate and share the infectious rhythms and joyous spirit of the music.

4. Music Halls and Theaters: Samba performances also take place in dedicated music halls and theaters, providing a platform for professional samba musicians and ensembles to showcase their artistry and entertain diverse audiences.

5. Local Bars and Clubs: Samba can be enjoyed in the intimate and vibrant ambiance of local bars and clubs, where live performances and jam sessions create an immersive and engaging musical experience for patrons and music enthusiasts alike.

The instruments used in samba and the diverse venues in which it is performed reflect the genre's dynamic and communal nature, emphasizing its role as a vibrant and integral part of Brazilian cultural expression and celebration.

§

Samba and Carnival

Samba and Carnival share a deeply intertwined relationship that forms the heart of Brazil's cultural identity and national heritage. Carnival, a vibrant and extravagant festival, represents a culmination of Brazilian traditions, folklore, and artistic expressions, with samba serving as its pulsating soundtrack. For a reader unfamiliar with this cultural phenomenon, here is a comprehensive exploration of the relationship between samba and Carnival, along with an introduction to Carnival itself:

Carnival: An Introduction

Carnival is an annual festival celebrated in various countries around the world, but it finds its most exuberant and elaborate manifestation in Brazil. The Brazilian Carnival is a multi-day event that typically takes place before Lent, marking a period of revelry, indulgence, and communal celebration. It is characterized by vibrant parades, elaborate costumes, exuberant music, and exultant street parties that captivate the entire nation. This festive extravaganza serves as a time for people to come together, shed inhibitions, and revel in the rich tapestry of Brazilian culture, music, and dance.

The Relationship between Samba and Carnival

Samba is at the heart of the Brazilian Carnival, serving as the rhythmic and melodic pulse that animates the festivities and drives the vibrant parades and street celebrations. The infectious beats, lively melodies, and spirited lyrics of samba music create an immersive and joyous atmosphere, inspiring participants and spectators alike to join in the energetic dance and revelry.

During Carnival, samba takes center stage through the elaborate performances of samba schools, which are community-based organizations dedicated to preserving and promoting the art of samba. These samba schools participate in competitive parades, known as "samba parades," where they showcase their intricate choreography, dazzling costumes, and synchronized musical arrangements to captivate audiences and judges.

The samba parades feature a dynamic display of vibrant floats, elaborate costumes adorned with feathers and sequins, and synchronized movements that reflect the cultural themes and narratives chosen by each samba school. These parades are a visual and auditory spectacle, where the rich heritage of Brazil comes alive through the rhythmic beats of samba music, the energetic dance performances, and the exuberant expressions of communal spirit and cultural pride.

The relationship between samba and Carnival is a testament to the cultural significance of music and dance in uniting communities, expressing shared values, and fostering a sense of collective identity. It represents a dynamic fusion of tradition and innovation, where the vibrant rhythms of samba serve as a powerful medium for storytelling, cultural expression, and the celebration of Brazil's diverse cultural heritage during the festive spirit of Carnival.

§

II. The Social and Political Context of Samba in Brazil

Samba, the rhythmic heartbeat of Brazilian culture, has deep-rooted socio-political implications that reflect the intricate tapestry of Brazil's history, culture, and identity. From its origins in the marginalized communities of Rio de Janeiro to its global recognition as a symbol of Brazilian cultural heritage, samba has been shaped by a complex interplay of social and political dynamics that have left an indelible mark on its evolution.

The colonial legacy and the enduring impact of slavery cast a profound shadow over the social fabric of Brazil, influencing the development of samba as a form of cultural resistance and resilience among Afro-Brazilian communities. The rhythmic structures and percussive elements of samba bear the imprint of African musical traditions, serving as a poignant reminder of the cultural hybridity and the enduring legacy of the African diaspora within Brazil's socio-cultural landscape.

As Brazil underwent urbanization and rapid industrialization, the emergence of samba as a popular musical genre paralleled the marginalization of Afro-Brazilian and lower-income communities within urban centers. Samba became a means of reclaiming cultural identity and fostering a sense of solidarity within marginalized groups, serving as a powerful medium for expressing the joys, struggles, and aspirations of a disenfranchised population.

The cultural hybridity inherent in samba's rhythmic and melodic compositions reflects the intricate interplay between African, European, and indigenous cultural elements, signifying the complex process of cultural assimilation and identity formation within the Brazilian context. Samba stands as a testament to Brazil's rich cultural diversity, serving as a powerful symbol of cultural nationalism and a source of national pride that transcends racial and socio-economic boundaries.

Despite its cultural significance, samba faced instances of censorship and political repression during periods of authoritarian rule in Brazil. However, samba also emerged as a form of political activism and social commentary, enabling musicians and artists to voice dissent against social injustices and advocate for political change, thereby demonstrating the resilience and transformative power of music in challenging the status quo.

Moreover, the global dissemination of samba as a cultural export has played a pivotal role in shaping Brazil's international image and promoting cross-cultural exchange on the global stage. Samba's infectious rhythms and vibrant melodies have served as a potent tool for cultural diplomacy, fostering international dialogue, and positioning Brazil as a dynamic and culturally vibrant nation with a rich musical heritage that continues to captivate audiences worldwide.

In essence, the social and political context of samba represents a poignant narrative of cultural resilience, identity formation, and socio-political transformation within the complex tapestry of

Brazilian history. Samba's enduring legacy as a powerful medium for cultural expression, social activism, and global cultural diplomacy stands as a testament to its enduring significance as a symbol of Brazilian cultural heritage and a vibrant reflection of the nation's rich and diverse cultural mosaic.

Suggested Reading

here is a list of books that could be useful in your research on Samba, Samba artists, Samba record labels, and the cultural history during the Golden Age of Samba:

- "The Brazilian Sound: Samba, Bossa Nova, and the Popular Music of Brazil" by Chris McGowan and Ricardo Pessanha.

- "Samba: Resistance in Motion" by Barbara Browning.

- "The Samba and the Mysterious World of Afro-Brazilian Music" by Alma Guillermoprieto.

- "Brazil: Five Centuries of Change" by Thomas E. Skidmore.

- "The Brazil Reader: History, Culture, Politics" edited by Robert M. Levine and John J. Crocitti.

These books should provide a comprehensive understanding of Samba's cultural significance, the history of Samba in Brazil, and the context surrounding the Golden Age of Samba.

Chapter 4. The Rise of Bossa Nova

Context: The 1950s in Brazil

The 1950s in Brazil marked a transformative era characterized by significant cultural, social, and political changes that shaped the country's trajectory and identity. Several key factors contributed to this transformation:

1. Economic Growth and Industrialization:
Brazil experienced substantial economic growth and industrial development during the 1950s. The government implemented policies that encouraged industrialization, leading to the expansion of manufacturing sectors such as steel, automotive, and petrochemical industries. This growth fostered urbanization and the rise of a burgeoning middle class, contributing to a shift in cultural dynamics and consumer patterns.

2. Political Stability and Democratization:
The 1950s saw a period of relative political stability and the consolidation of democratic institutions in Brazil. This stability provided a conducive environment for social and cultural movements to flourish, fostering a sense of optimism and cultural renaissance among the populace.

3. Cultural Renaissance and Modernization:
The 1950s marked a cultural renaissance in Brazil, characterized by a revival of artistic expression, literary movements, and musical innovation. This era witnessed a flourishing of Brazilian literature, music, and cinema, as artists and intellectuals sought to redefine the national cultural identity and establish Brazil as a hub for artistic creativity and intellectual discourse.

4. Rise of National Identity and Cultural Pride:
The period saw a renewed emphasis on fostering a sense of national identity and cultural pride. Brazil sought to assert its unique cultural heritage on the global stage, leading to a

resurgence of interest in traditional Brazilian music, literature, and folklore. This cultural revival contributed to a sense of unity and shared identity among Brazilians, fostering a spirit of nationalism and cultural celebration.

5. Social Movements and Identity Politics:
The 1950s witnessed the emergence of social movements advocating for the rights of marginalized communities, including Afro-Brazilians and indigenous populations. These movements played a crucial role in highlighting issues of social inequality, racial discrimination, and cultural marginalization, paving the way for a more inclusive and diverse cultural landscape in Brazil.

Overall, the transformative nature of the 1950s in Brazil can be attributed to the confluence of economic development, political stability, cultural resurgence, and social activism, all of which contributed to the shaping of Brazil's modern identity and cultural landscape.

I. Defining Bossa Nova

Bossa Nova (noun):

1. A style of Brazilian music originating in the late 1950s.
2. Derived from samba, with an emphasis on melody and subdued percussion.
3. Known for its smooth, laid-back rhythms, and subtle, sophisticated harmonies.
4. Often characterized by intimate vocals, intricate guitar playing, and a focus on romantic and everyday themes.
5. Gained international prominence in the 1960s, contributing to the global appreciation of Brazilian music and culture.

Bossa Nova is a genre of Brazilian music that emerged in the late 1950s and gained international prominence in the 1960s. Characterized by its distinctive blend of samba rhythms, jazz influences, and sophisticated melodic structures, Bossa Nova is known for its laid-back, smooth, and subtly syncopated musical style. It is often characterized by its intimate and expressive vocals, intricate guitar playing, and understated yet rich harmonies. Bossa Nova's lyrical themes frequently revolve around love, longing, and the beauty of everyday life, reflecting a sense of urban sophistication and romanticism. It represents a significant contribution to the global music landscape, capturing the essence of Brazilian musical elegance and cultural allure.

§

In the transformative era of 1950s Brazil, a convergence of cultural, social, and political dynamics set the stage for the emergence of Bossa Nova. Against the backdrop of Brazil's burgeoning urban centers, the country was undergoing a period of rapid modernization and cultural renaissance. The effervescent energy of post-war optimism, coupled with a growing sense of national identity, contributed to a thriving artistic climate that fostered innovation and experimentation in music, literature, and the arts.

Amidst this cultural renaissance, Brazil grappled with socioeconomic disparities and a quest for identity, providing fertile ground for musical expression to encapsulate the complexities of the Brazilian experience. The burgeoning middle class, with its newfound affluence and cosmopolitan aspirations, sought a musical sound that would reflect their aspirations and experiences, leading to the rise of a new musical movement that would come to be known as Bossa Nova.

Influences from Samba, Jazz, and Other Music Genres

Bossa Nova, in its embryonic stage, drew inspiration from a diverse array of musical genres, including the rhythmic intricacies of traditional samba, the harmonic sophistication of jazz, and the lyrical poignancy of Brazilian folk music. The fusion of these influences yielded a unique musical language that emphasized intricate melodies, subtle harmonies, and a distinct rhythmic pulse, setting Bossa Nova apart from its predecessors.

80

The syncopated rhythms of samba, characterized by their infectious energy and pulsating beats, provided the foundation upon which Bossa Nova built its rhythmic framework, infusing the genre with a sense of Brazilian authenticity and cultural resonance. Jazz, with its improvisational spirit and harmonic complexities, contributed to the sophisticated musical arrangements and nuanced chord progressions that defined the melodic landscape of Bossa Nova, imbuing it with a refined and cosmopolitan allure that transcended national borders.

The Emergence of Bossa Nova in the Urban Neighborhoods of Rio de Janeiro

Bossa Nova found its genesis in the vibrant and eclectic neighborhoods of Rio de Janeiro, where a community of young musicians, artists, and intellectuals converged to shape the artistic narrative of the era. The beachside neighborhoods of Ipanema and Copacabana, along with the bohemian enclaves of Botafogo and Leme, served as creative hubs where musicians such as João Gilberto, Antônio Carlos Jobim, and Vinícius de Moraes collaborated and honed the distinctive sound of Bossa Nova.

In the intimate bars and cafés of Rio's urban landscape, the melodious strains of Bossa Nova began to captivate audiences, encapsulating the essence of romance, melancholy, and poetic introspection that resonated with the aspirations and sensibilities of the burgeoning middle class. The simplicity of its melodies, the intimacy of its lyrics, and the understated elegance of its musical arrangements captured the essence of a new Brazilian aesthetic, marking the dawn of a musical movement that would revolutionize the global perception of Brazilian music and culture.

II. Key Innovators and Early Exponents

The early development of Bossa Nova was shaped by the contributions of several key innovators and artists who played instrumental roles in defining the genre's distinctive sound and fostering its global recognition. Some of the notable figures and early exponents of Bossa Nova include:

1. João Gilberto (1931-2019): Often regarded as the pioneer of Bossa Nova, João Gilberto's innovative guitar playing style and intimate vocal delivery were pivotal in defining the genre's characteristic sound. His seminal recordings, such as "Chega de Saudade" and "Desafinado," showcased his unique approach to rhythm and phrasing, laying the foundation for the emergence of Bossa Nova in the late 1950s.

2. Antônio Carlos Jobim (1927-1994): Renowned for his exceptional skills as a composer, pianist, and arranger, Antônio Carlos Jobim was a central figure in the development of Bossa Nova. His sophisticated harmonic sensibilities and lyrical compositions, including classics like "The Girl from Ipanema" and "Corcovado," contributed to the genre's international success and solidified its reputation as a refined and cosmopolitan musical style.

3. Vinícius de Moraes (1913-1980): A celebrated poet, lyricist, and composer, Vinícius de Moraes collaborated closely with Jobim and other musicians to create some of the most enduring and poetic Bossa Nova compositions. His lyrical depth and romantic sensibilities added a profound layer of introspection and emotion to the genre, elevating its thematic richness and cultural resonance.

4. Carlos Lyra (b. 1939): A prominent singer and songwriter, Carlos Lyra was a key figure in the early Bossa Nova movement, known for his contributions to the evolution of the genre's lyrical themes and musical arrangements. His compositions, such as "Influência do Jazz" and "Você e Eu," reflected a fusion of Bossa Nova with jazz influences, contributing to the genre's dynamic and diverse musical landscape.

These early exponents and innovators of Bossa Nova played a foundational role in shaping the genre's artistic trajectory, fostering its global recognition, and establishing its enduring legacy as a quintessential expression of Brazilian musical elegance and cultural sophistication.

§

Focus: "The Girl from Ipanema"

Conception and Original Recording

"The Girl from Ipanema" (Garota de Ipanema) stands as one of the most iconic and globally recognized Bossa Nova compositions, with music by Antônio Carlos Jobim and Portuguese lyrics by Vinícius de Moraes. The song was inspired by the ethereal beauty of Heloísa Eneida Menezes Paes Pinto, a young woman from Rio de Janeiro's Ipanema neighborhood, whose graceful presence captivated the composers as she strolled past the Veloso bar.

The song's 1962 original recording, featuring João Gilberto's intimate vocals and Astrud Gilberto's understated yet alluring English verses, epitomized the essence of Bossa Nova's laid-back rhythms, sophisticated harmonies, and intimate storytelling.

Remakes and Global Influence

"The Girl from Ipanema" has undergone numerous remakes and reinterpretations by artists from diverse musical backgrounds, transcending cultural and linguistic barriers to become a cross-genre and cross-cultural phenomenon.

From Frank Sinatra and Ella Fitzgerald's timeless renditions to contemporary covers by artists such as Amy Winehouse and Madonna, the song's enduring appeal has cemented its status as a beloved classic in the global musical canon. Its crossover appeal has facilitated its integration into various genres, including jazz, pop, and easy listening, underscoring its ability to transcend musical boundaries and resonate with audiences across generations.

Legacy and Cultural Significance

"The Girl from Ipanema" has left an indelible mark on the cultural landscape, symbolizing the epitome of Brazilian musical elegance and poetic storytelling. Its portrayal of unrequited love, yearning, and the fleeting beauty of youth has resonated with audiences worldwide, capturing the romantic allure of Rio de Janeiro's Ipanema beach and immortalizing the image of the enigmatic girl who inspired its creation.

The song's legacy extends beyond its musical accolades, serving as a cultural ambassador for Brazil, evoking images of sun-kissed beaches, swaying palm trees, and the rhythmic pulse of Bossa Nova, thereby perpetuating Brazil's image as a hub of cultural sophistication and natural beauty.

Relationship to Other Genres and Global Musical Influence

"The Girl from Ipanema" has had a profound impact on the global music landscape, influencing the development of various musical genres and fostering cross-cultural collaborations that have enriched the tapestry of international music.

Its fusion of Bossa Nova's melodic grace with jazz-infused harmonies has inspired artists worldwide to incorporate elements of Brazilian musical aesthetics into their own compositions, contributing to the diversification and hybridization of musical styles.

Moreover, its cross-cultural resonance has underscored the universal appeal of Bossa Nova, fostering a deeper appreciation for Brazilian music and culture across diverse cultural and geographical contexts.

Jazz Details

Certainly, "The Girl from Ipanema" is a well-known Bossa Nova and jazz standard. The song features a distinct Bossa Nova rhythm, and its melody allows for various jazz interpretations and phrasing. While the song's phrasing can vary depending on the performer and the specific rendition, here is a general guide to the jazz phrasing in "The Girl from Ipanema":

1. Syncopation: Emphasize the syncopated rhythms in the melody, particularly during the verses, to capture the laid-back, swaying feel of the Bossa Nova style.

2. Melodic Punctuation: Highlight the melodic punctuation, such as the pauses and accents on certain notes, to bring out the subtle nuances of the melody.

3. Swing Feel: Infuse a subtle swing feel into the phrasing, particularly during instrumental solos and improvisational sections, to incorporate the jazz element into the performance.

4. Expressive Dynamics: Employ expressive dynamics, including crescendos and decrescendos, to add depth and emotion to the phrasing, enhancing the overall musical storytelling.

5. Subtle Ornamentation: Incorporate subtle ornamentation, such as trills, grace notes, and melodic embellishments, to add flair and personality to the interpretation, while remaining true to the song's Bossa Nova roots.

When performing or interpreting "The Girl from Ipanema" in a jazz context, it is essential to maintain the song's inherent Bossa Nova rhythm while incorporating elements of jazz phrasing to create a nuanced and engaging musical performance.

Suggested Listening

Original Recording: "The Girl from Ipanema"

Original Artists: Stan Getz, João Gilberto, and Astrud Gilberto
Year of Release: 1964
Label: Verve Records

Listening Notes:
- The original recording features the enchanting vocals of João Gilberto and the ethereal English verses sung by Astrud Gilberto, creating an intimate and romantic atmosphere.
- The gentle sway of the Bossa Nova rhythm, accompanied by João Gilberto's delicate guitar playing and Stan Getz's evocative saxophone melodies, captures the essence of the Ipanema beach's languid charm.
- Astrud Gilberto's soft, evocative delivery of the English verses, infused with a touch of melancholic longing, beautifully complements the song's wistful narrative and lyrical imagery.
- The seamless interplay between the Brazilian and American musicians showcases the cross-cultural collaboration that defined the global appeal of Bossa Nova in the 1960s.

Top 5 Remakes:

1. Frank Sinatra and Antônio Carlos Jobim (1967) - Sinatra's rendition infuses the song with his signature vocal charisma, complemented by Jobim's lush orchestral arrangement, creating an enchanting blend of American and Brazilian musical sensibilities.

2. Ella Fitzgerald (1967) - Fitzgerald's rendition showcases her unparalleled vocal virtuosity, infusing the song with her dynamic vocal range and improvisational prowess, offering a fresh interpretation while honoring the song's inherent elegance.

3. Amy Winehouse (2002) - Winehouse's soulful and emotive rendition imbues the song with a contemporary edge, blending elements of jazz and R&B to offer a modern reinterpretation that pays homage to the timeless allure of the original composition.

4. Diana Krall (2009) - Krall's rendition exudes a captivating intimacy, emphasizing the song's romantic essence with her velvety vocals and subtle piano accompaniment, infusing the melody with a sense of quiet introspection and emotional depth.

5. Stan Getz and Astrud Gilberto (1975) - This rendition, featuring one of the original artists, maintains the nostalgic charm of the original recording while offering a nuanced interpretation that highlights the enduring appeal of the song's timeless melody and evocative storytelling.

Focus: João Gilberto

At the time of recording "The Girl from Ipanema," João Gilberto was a revered figure in the world of Brazilian music, renowned for his pioneering role in popularizing Bossa Nova and his innovative approach to guitar playing and vocal delivery. His intimate and nuanced interpretation of the genre, characterized by its rhythmic intricacies and understated elegance, helped define the essence of Bossa Nova and solidify its position as a globally recognized musical style.

Following the success of "The Girl from Ipanema" and the international acclaim garnered by the Bossa Nova movement, João Gilberto continued to exert a profound influence on the trajectory of Brazilian music, collaborating with prominent artists and contributing to the genre's enduring legacy. His subsequent recordings and live performances showcased his continued dedication to refining the subtleties of Bossa Nova, emphasizing the genre's introspective lyricism and harmonic sophistication.

Despite facing personal challenges and experiencing periods of seclusion in his later years, João Gilberto's musical legacy remained a testament to his unwavering commitment to artistic excellence and his pivotal role in shaping the Brazilian musical landscape. His innovative guitar style, distinctive vocal phrasing, and contributions to the evolution of Bossa Nova solidified his status as a true icon of Brazilian music, earning him a place among the most influential and revered musicians of the 20th century.

João Gilberto's profound impact on the global appreciation of Brazilian music and his enduring legacy as a trailblazing figure in the realm of Bossa Nova continue to resonate with audiences worldwide, reaffirming his status as a cultural luminary whose musical contributions transcend time and cultural boundaries.

Focus: Antônio Carlos Jobim

Antônio Carlos Jobim, often referred to as the "father of Bossa Nova," was a Brazilian composer, pianist, songwriter, arranger, and singer who made significant contributions to the development and popularization of the Bossa Nova genre. His musical innovations and artistic vision played a pivotal role in shaping the sound and identity of Brazilian music on the global stage. Here is a comprehensive overview of his contributions to composition and arrangement within the realm of Bossa Nova:

1. Innovative Compositional Style: Jobim's compositions were characterized by their sophisticated harmonies, rich melodies, and poetic lyricism. He often incorporated elements of jazz, classical, and traditional Brazilian music into his works, creating a unique and captivating fusion of musical styles.

2. Iconic Songwriting: Jobim was renowned for his timeless and iconic compositions, including "The Girl from Ipanema," "Corcovado," and "Desafinado," which became some of the most recognizable and enduring classics in the Bossa Nova repertoire. His lyrical themes often celebrated the beauty of nature, love, and the essence of Brazilian culture, resonating with audiences worldwide.

3. Harmonic Exploration: Jobim's compositions showcased intricate harmonic progressions and nuanced chord structures, demonstrating his mastery of complex musical arrangements and his ability to infuse traditional Brazilian music with contemporary jazz elements. His harmonic explorations contributed to the development of the distinctive sound and emotional depth that defined Bossa Nova music.

4. Collaborations and Partnerships: Jobim collaborated with several prominent musicians and vocalists, such as João Gilberto, Stan Getz, and Frank Sinatra, among others, contributing to the popularization of Bossa Nova internationally. His collaborations not only highlighted his exceptional talent as a composer and arranger but also showcased his ability to adapt the Bossa Nova style to accommodate diverse musical sensibilities and cultural contexts.

5. Orchestration and Arrangement Techniques: Jobim's expertise in orchestration and arrangement was evident in his meticulous attention to detail and his ability to craft intricate musical textures and layers within his compositions. His innovative use of instrumentation, including the guitar, piano, and orchestral arrangements, added depth and richness to the Bossa Nova sound, elevating it to new heights of sophistication and artistry.

6. Global Impact and Legacy: Jobim's profound influence on the development of Bossa Nova transcended cultural boundaries and continues to resonate with musicians and audiences worldwide. His contributions to composition and arrangement not only shaped the trajectory of Brazilian music but also left an indelible mark on the history of contemporary jazz and popular music, solidifying his legacy as one of the most influential and celebrated figures in the world of music.

The Influential 10: Bossa Nova

1. João Gilberto:

Unique Contributions: Pioneered the rhythmic guitar style integral to Bossa Nova and popularized the genre internationally.

Biography: Born in Brazil, Gilberto's innovative guitar-playing and soft vocal style defined the essence of Bossa Nova.

Essential Recordings: "Chega de Saudade" (1959), "Desafinado" (1962), "O Amor, O Sorriso e a Flor" (1960).
Influences: Influenced by Brazilian samba and jazz music, particularly the works of Antonio Carlos Jobim and Dorival Caymmi.

Legacy: Known for revolutionizing Brazilian music, Gilberto's legacy remains a cornerstone of Bossa Nova's global recognition and influence.

2. Vinicius de Moraes:

Unique Contributions: Renowned for his poetic lyrics and collaborations with prominent Bossa Nova composers and musicians.

Biography: A Brazilian poet, playwright, and diplomat, de Moraes was instrumental in shaping the lyrical essence of Bossa Nova.

Essential Recordings: "Maria Bethânia" (1965), "Vinicius + Bethânia + Toquinho + Miúcha" (1975), "Vinicius & Toquinho" (1975).

Influences: Influenced by Brazilian folk music, classical poetry, and the works of international poets such as Federico García Lorca and Pablo Neruda.

Legacy: Remembered for his profound impact on the poetic and lyrical dimensions of Bossa Nova, de Moraes' contributions continue to inspire contemporary Brazilian songwriters and poets.

3. Stan Getz:

Unique Contributions: Renowned American jazz saxophonist who popularized Bossa Nova in the United States and globally.

Biography: Born in the U.S., Getz's collaborations with Brazilian musicians helped introduce Bossa Nova to a broader international audience.

Essential Recordings: "Getz/Gilberto" (1964), "Big Band Bossa Nova" (1962), "Stan Getz Plays" (1952).

Influences: Influenced by the bebop and cool jazz movements, as well as prominent American saxophonists like Lester Young and Zoot Sims.

Legacy: Recognized for his pivotal role in popularizing Bossa Nova outside of Brazil, Getz's contributions bridged the gap between Brazilian and American jazz traditions.

4. Tom Jobim:

Unique Contributions: Noted for his compositions and arrangements that defined the harmonic and melodic richness of Bossa Nova.

Biography: A Brazilian composer, pianist, and songwriter, Jobim's works epitomized the soul of Bossa Nova music.

Essential Recordings: "Wave" (1967), "Stone Flower" (1970), "Antonio Carlos Jobim and Friends" (1996).

Influences: Influenced by Brazilian folk music, classical composers like Johann Sebastian Bach, and American jazz musicians such as George Gershwin and Duke Ellington.

Legacy: Revered as one of the most influential figures in the history of Bossa Nova, Jobim's compositions and arrangements continue to shape the trajectory of Brazilian and global music.

5. Elis Regina:

Unique Contributions: Celebrated for her powerful vocal delivery and interpretations of Bossa Nova classics, showcasing a blend of passion and technical prowess.

Biography: A Brazilian singer known for her dynamic stage presence and emotionally charged performances of Bossa Nova and Música Popular Brasileira (MPB).

Essential Recordings: "Elis & Tom" (1974), "Elis Regina in London" (1969), "Elis" (1973).

Influences: Influenced by a diverse array of Brazilian and international vocalists, including Billie Holiday, Ella Fitzgerald, and Maysa.

Legacy: Regarded as one of the most influential and beloved Brazilian vocalists, Regina's interpretations of Bossa Nova classics continue to inspire contemporary singers and musicians globally.

6. Carlos Lyra:

Unique Contributions: Noted for his contributions to the early development of Bossa Nova and his collaborations with other influential figures in the genre.

Biography: A Brazilian singer-songwriter and guitarist, Lyra's melodic sensibilities and rhythmic innovations were instrumental in shaping the early sound of Bossa Nova.

Essential Recordings: "Carlos Lyra" (1959), "Depois do Carnaval" (2002), "Eu e a Brisa" (1960).

Influences: Influenced by Brazilian samba, jazz, and American songwriters like Cole Porter and George Gershwin.

Legacy: Recognized for his enduring contributions to the development of Bossa Nova, Lyra's compositions and collaborations continue to be celebrated as cornerstones of the genre's rich musical heritage.

7. Nara Leão:

Unique Contributions: Known for her role in popularizing Bossa Nova through her interpretations of classic songs and her advocacy for emerging Brazilian songwriters.

Biography: A Brazilian singer and political activist, Leão's introspective vocal style and socially conscious lyrics exemplified the spirit of Bossa Nova's cultural and artistic expression.

Essential Recordings: "Nara" (1964), "Opinião de Nara" (1964), "Coisas do Mundo" (1976).

Influences: Influenced by Brazilian folk music, contemporary poets, and the emerging political and social movements in Brazil during the 1960s.

Legacy: Remembered for her contributions to the popularization of Bossa Nova and her commitment to using music as a tool for social and political change, Leão's legacy remains deeply intertwined with the cultural and historical fabric of Brazil.

8. Roberto Menescal:

Unique Contributions: Celebrated for his role as a guitarist, composer, and arranger, shaping the instrumental and melodic dimensions of Bossa Nova.

Biography: A Brazilian musician and producer, Menescal's melodic guitar playing and contributions to the arrangement of Bossa Nova compositions cemented his influence in the genre.

Essential Recordings: "Rio Bossa" (1962), "O Barquinho" (1965), "Bossa Nova Meets The Beatles" (2004).

Influences: Influenced by Brazilian Bossa Nova and samba, as well as the emerging international musical trends of the 1950s and 1960s.

Legacy: Recognized as a key figure in the development and popularization of Bossa Nova, Menescal's instrumental prowess and compositional ingenuity continue to inspire generations of Brazilian musicians and guitarists.

9. Sérgio Mendes:

Unique Contributions: Celebrated for his pioneering work in popularizing Bossa Nova and Brazilian music on the international stage through his innovative blends with jazz and pop.

Biography: A Brazilian pianist, composer, and bandleader, Mendes' fusion of Bossa Nova with elements of jazz and pop redefined the genre's global appeal.

Essential Recordings: "Brasil '66" (1966), "Look Around" (1968), "The Swinger from Rio" (1964).

Influences: Influenced by Brazilian samba, American jazz, and contemporary pop music, as well as the vibrant cultural scene of 1960s Brazil.

Legacy: Recognized for his role in introducing Bossa Nova to international audiences and his pioneering efforts in blending Brazilian rhythms with global musical sensibilities, Mendes' influence continues to resonate across diverse musical genres and cultures worldwide.

10. Luiz Bonfá:

Unique Contributions: Renowned for his innovative guitar work and influential compositions that contributed to the evolution of Bossa Nova.

Biography: A Brazilian guitarist and composer, Bonfá's dynamic guitar style and intricate melodies were instrumental in shaping the sound of early Bossa Nova.

Essential Recordings: "Amor! The Fabulous Guitar of Luiz Bonfá" (1963), "The Brazilian Scene" (1965), "Solo in Rio 1959" (2005).

Influences: Influenced by a combination of classical music, Brazilian samba, and American jazz guitarists such as Django Reinhardt and Charlie Christian.

Legacy: Remembered for his significant contributions to the development of Bossa Nova's guitar language and his enduring influence on subsequent generations of Brazilian and international guitarists.

§

Musical Characteristics and Innovations in Bossa Nova have significantly contributed to the genre's distinct identity and enduring appeal. Some examples:

A. Rhythmic and Harmonic Elements:

- Bossa Nova's rhythmic foundation is characterized by syncopated beats, intricate guitar patterns, and subtle percussion, creating a laid-back, yet vibrant, groove.

- Harmonically, Bossa Nova integrates sophisticated jazz harmonies, including extended chords, altered dominants, and subtle modulations, infusing the music with a rich and nuanced tonal palette.

- The fusion of samba rhythms with jazz harmonies gives Bossa Nova its signature blend of infectious energy and melodic complexity, setting it apart from other contemporary music genres.

B. Evolution of Lyrical Themes and Songwriting Style:

- Early Bossa Nova songs often explored themes of romance, love, and the beauty of nature, reflecting an optimistic and poetic sensibility deeply rooted in Brazilian culture.

- Over time, the lyrical themes expanded to include social commentary, political reflections, and introspective narratives, capturing the changing socio-cultural landscape of Brazil and addressing universal human experiences with a sense of depth and introspection.

- Bossa Nova's songwriting style is characterized by its melodic elegance, poetic lyricism, and a delicate balance between introspection and social commentary, creating a profound emotional resonance that transcends linguistic and cultural boundaries.

C. Role of Instrumentation and Arrangements:

- The use of classical and jazz instrumentation, including guitars, pianos, flutes, and drums, played a pivotal role in defining the sophisticated and refined sound of Bossa Nova.

- Instrumental arrangements in Bossa Nova are characterized by intricate melodic lines, subtle counterpoint, and the interplay of various instrumental voices, contributing to the genre's lush and textured musical tapestry.

- The incorporation of string sections, brass arrangements, and nuanced percussive elements adds depth and complexity to the overall musical arrangement, enhancing the expressive dynamics and tonal richness of Bossa Nova compositions.

The intricate interplay of rhythmic and harmonic elements, the evolution of lyrical themes and songwriting style, and the strategic use of instrumentation and arrangements collectively define the captivating and timeless allure of Bossa Nova, solidifying its place as one of the most revered and influential music genres in the global musical landscape.

IV. Bossa Nova's Impact on Brazilian Society

Bossa Nova's Impact on Brazilian Society was multi-faceted, influencing the country's cultural, social, and global identity. Here is a brief exploration of its impact:

Social and Cultural Implications of Bossa Nova's Rise:

- Bossa Nova's emergence coincided with a period of cultural renaissance and social transformation in Brazil, providing a musical backdrop to a society grappling with political shifts and modernization.

- The genre's emphasis on poetic lyricism, intimate narratives, and sophisticated melodies offered a new artistic language that resonated with the intellectual and artistic circles, fostering a sense of cultural pride and artistic reawakening.

Reflections on the Genre's Connection to Changing Society

- Bossa Nova's lyrical themes often echoed the spirit of a changing Brazilian society, addressing themes of urbanization, love, longing, and the complex realities of modern life, reflecting the aspirations, struggles, and complexities of the Brazilian people during the mid-20th century.

- The genre's introspective and contemplative nature mirrored the cultural shifts and evolving values of a society in transition, providing a nuanced artistic commentary on the changing social fabric of Brazil.

Bossa Nova's Role in Reshaping Brazil's Global Identity

- Bossa Nova's global popularity served as a powerful vehicle for reshaping Brazil's cultural identity on the international stage, presenting the country as a hub of musical innovation and cultural richness.

- The genre's fusion of Brazilian musical traditions with global influences helped redefine perceptions of Brazilian culture beyond traditional stereotypes, showcasing Brazil as a dynamic and sophisticated cultural force, influencing artistic trends and perceptions of Latin American culture worldwide.

Bossa Nova's profound impact on Brazilian society extended beyond its musical contributions, shaping the country's cultural narrative and global identity, and leaving an enduring legacy that continues to inspire artistic expressions and cultural dialogues within Brazil and beyond.

§

There were several contemporary artists and bands who were known for carrying forward the legacy of Bossa Nova, infusing the genre with their own modern interpretations. While I might not have specific information on developments after 2021, here are some artists and bands who were known for their work in the genre up until that time:

1. Bebel Gilberto: Daughter of Bossa Nova legend João Gilberto, Bebel Gilberto has continued the family tradition and has become an important figure in contemporary Bossa Nova. She has managed to blend traditional Bossa Nova with modern sounds, incorporating electronic elements into her music.

2. Celso Fonseca: Fonseca is known for his smooth voice and guitar playing, and he has made significant contributions to the modern Bossa Nova scene. His music often blends traditional Brazilian rhythms with jazz and contemporary styles.

3. Céu: While not strictly a Bossa Nova artist, Céu has drawn influence from the genre in her music. Her work often blends Bossa Nova with electronic, reggae, and other global influences, creating a unique and modern sound.

4. Vinicius Cantuária: A Brazilian guitarist, singer, and composer, Cantuária has contributed to the development of modern Bossa Nova. His music often includes elements of jazz, pop, and Bossa Nova, creating a fusion that appeals to contemporary audiences.

5. Rosa Passos: Passos is known for her unique interpretations of Bossa Nova classics as well as her original compositions. She has maintained the essence of traditional Bossa Nova while incorporating her own distinct style and musical influences.

6. Thievery Corporation: While not solely a Bossa Nova band, Thievery Corporation has incorporated elements of the genre into their music. They are known for their eclectic style, blending various genres such as electronic, dub, and world music, including Bossa Nova influences in some of their tracks.

These artists and bands have contributed significantly to keeping the spirit of Bossa Nova alive while infusing it with contemporary elements. There may be additional artists who have emerged since my last update, so I recommend exploring recent music platforms and websites to discover more contemporary Bossa Nova artists.

§

Bossa Nova, with its smooth rhythms, gentle melodies, and poetic lyrics, has left an indelible mark on the music world since its emergence in the late 1950s. Its enduring legacy can be attributed to several key factors:

1. Timeless Appeal: The genre's timeless appeal lies in its ability to evoke a sense of relaxation, romance, and nostalgia. Its gentle melodies and soothing rhythms create an atmosphere of tranquility that continues to resonate with audiences across generations.

2. Influence on Global Music: Bossa Nova's influence extends far beyond its Brazilian origins, impacting genres such as jazz, pop, and world music. Its unique blend of samba rhythms and jazz harmonies has inspired countless musicians worldwide, leading to the creation of various fusion genres.

3. Musical Innovation and Fusion: The genre encourages musical experimentation and fusion, allowing artists to infuse Bossa Nova with elements from diverse musical traditions. This adaptability has enabled Bossa Nova to remain relevant and appealing to contemporary audiences.

For a new musician, creating within the Bossa Nova genre can offer several enticing prospects/

1. Exploration of Musical Fusion: Bossa Nova provides a platform for blending traditional Brazilian rhythms with contemporary styles, allowing musicians to experiment with a wide range of musical influences and create something entirely fresh and unique.

2. Emotional Expression and Intimacy: The genre's emphasis on lyrical storytelling and intimate melodies provides a space for musicians to convey their emotions and experiences in a heartfelt manner, fostering a deep connection with their audience.

3. Cultural Connection and Heritage: Creating within the Bossa Nova genre allows musicians to honor and preserve Brazil's rich musical heritage while also contributing to its ongoing evolution, thereby ensuring that the genre continues to thrive and remain relevant in the contemporary music landscape.

In the context of a contemporary world marked by discord and turmoil, Bossa Nova can serve as a soothing balm, offering a momentary escape from the chaos and inviting listeners to experience moments of serenity and introspection. Its calming melodies and nostalgic undertones can provide solace, fostering a sense of unity and understanding that transcends cultural and societal divisions.

Moreover, Bossa Nova's emphasis on storytelling and emotional expression can serve as a powerful tool for fostering empathy and understanding, encouraging individuals to reflect on shared human experiences and connect with one another on a deeper level. By embracing the genre's introspective nature, musicians can contribute to a collective musical narrative that promotes harmony, understanding, and peace in a world that often feels disjointed and tumultuous.

Chapter 5. The Rise of
Música Popular Brasileira (MPB)

Música Popular Brasileira (MPB) is a genre of Brazilian popular music that emerged in the late 1960s, characterized by its fusion of various musical styles such as samba, bossa nova, jazz, rock, and regional Brazilian folk music. MPB encompasses a wide range of musical expressions, including diverse rhythms, poetic lyrics, and intricate melodies that reflect Brazil's rich cultural heritage and societal complexities. It often serves as a vehicle for social and political commentary, addressing a variety of themes such as love, identity, social justice, and the cultural diversity of Brazil. MPB has played a significant role in shaping Brazilian cultural identity and has contributed to the country's vibrant and dynamic music scene, both domestically and internationally.

I. The Setting

The emergence of Música Popular Brasileira (MPB) in the 1960s was closely intertwined with the complex social and political landscape of Brazil during that period. Several key factors shaped the context within which MPB emerged, influencing its themes, lyrical content, and overall artistic expression. Some of the significant social and political contexts include:

1. Military Dictatorship and Censorship: The 1960s and 1970s in Brazil were marked by a military dictatorship that imposed strict censorship on various forms of artistic expression. As a result, many musicians turned to music as a means of expressing dissent and addressing social and political issues indirectly, often through metaphorical and allegorical lyrics.

2. Cultural Activism and Social Movements: The rise of various social movements, including the student movement and the workers' movement, fostered a climate of cultural activism and resistance. Many musicians aligned themselves with these movements, using their music as a tool for advocating social justice, human rights, and political change.

3. Urbanization and Social Change: The rapid urbanization and socio-economic transformations in Brazil during the 1960s influenced the themes explored in MPB. Musicians often depicted the challenges faced by urban dwellers, the disparities in society, and the struggles of marginalized communities, reflecting the broader social and economic changes occurring in the country.

4. Cultural Identity and Nationalism: MPB artists actively engaged with questions of Brazilian cultural identity and nationalism, drawing inspiration from the country's rich cultural heritage and diverse musical traditions. They sought to promote a sense of pride in Brazilian culture while also advocating for social inclusivity and equality among different social groups.

5. International Influences and Cross-Cultural Exchanges: Despite the restrictive political environment, Brazil was experiencing a period of increased global cultural exchange. MPB musicians were influenced by international musical trends, incorporating elements from jazz, rock, and other global genres, which enriched the diversity and complexity of the MPB sound.

In response to these social and political realities, the songs and lyrics of MPB often conveyed messages of social consciousness, political critique, and calls for social transformation. The genre served as a powerful medium for reflecting the aspirations and struggles of the Brazilian people, contributing to a collective consciousness that transcended the confines of the political climate and resonated with audiences both within Brazil and abroad.

Música Popular Brasileira (MPB) has long served as a potent vehicle for social change, activism, and cultural expression in Brazil. The genre has been deeply intertwined with the country's sociopolitical landscape, playing a pivotal role in reflecting the struggles, aspirations, and cultural identity of the Brazilian people.

A closer look at the socio-political narratives within MPB:

MPB as a Vehicle for Social Change and Activism:
MPB has often been used as a powerful tool for social critique and political activism. During periods of political repression, MPB artists utilized their music to express dissent and raise awareness about social injustices and human rights abuses. Through their lyrics and performances, they addressed issues such as poverty, inequality, and political oppression, advocating for social change and fostering a sense of collective consciousness among the Brazilian populace.

Role of MPB in Shaping Brazilian Cultural Identity:
MPB has played a central role in shaping and preserving Brazilian cultural identity. The genre draws upon diverse musical traditions, including samba, bossa nova, and regional folk music, reflecting the rich cultural heritage of Brazil. MPB artists have celebrated the country's cultural diversity through their music, emphasizing the importance of cultural inclusivity and unity. By promoting Brazilian cultural values and traditions, MPB has reinforced a sense of national pride and solidarity among Brazilians.

Evolution of Lyricism and Political Commentary in the Genre:
The evolution of lyricism within MPB has been characterized by a heightened emphasis on social and political commentary. MPB artists have utilized their lyrics to critique authoritarian regimes, highlight social disparities, and advocate for democratic values and human rights. Over the years, the genre has evolved to incorporate more nuanced and introspective lyrical themes, delving into personal struggles, love, and existential questions while still maintaining a strong undercurrent of social consciousness and political engagement.

By embracing these sociopolitical narratives, MPB has not only served as a form of artistic expression but has also played a crucial role in fostering social awareness, cultural pride, and democratic values within Brazilian society. Its ability to amplify marginalized voices and articulate the struggles of the disenfranchised has solidified its position as a powerful medium for advocating social change, promoting cultural understanding, and preserving the collective memory of the Brazilian people.

II. Early Innovators and Pioneers of the Genre

The early history of Música Popular Brasileira (MPB) is marked by the contributions of several pioneering artists who laid the groundwork for the genre's development and evolution. These innovators played a crucial role in shaping the musical landscape of Brazil and setting the stage for the emergence of MPB as a distinct and influential genre.

Some of the early innovators and pioneers of MPB include:

1. João Gilberto: Often referred to as the "Father of Bossa Nova," João Gilberto's innovative guitar playing and smooth vocal style were instrumental in popularizing the genre both in Brazil and internationally. His seminal album "Chega de Saudade" (1959) is considered a landmark recording in the history of Brazilian music.

2. Vinicius de Moraes: Renowned for his poetic lyrics and collaborations with prominent musicians such as Antonio Carlos Jobim and João Gilberto, Vinicius de Moraes was a key figure in the early development of Bossa Nova. His contributions to the genre helped shape its lyrical and melodic characteristics.

3. Antonio Carlos Jobim: A celebrated composer, pianist, and songwriter, Jobim was a central figure in the creation and popularization of Bossa Nova. His compositions, including the classic "The Girl from Ipanema," played a significant role in introducing Brazilian music to a global audience and establishing Bossa Nova as a prominent musical genre.

4. Elis Regina: Known for her powerful voice and dynamic stage presence, Elis Regina emerged as one of the leading voices of MPB in the 1960s and 1970s. Her interpretations of classic Brazilian songs and her collaborations with renowned songwriters contributed to the genre's growing popularity and cultural significance.

5. Milton Nascimento: With his unique blend of Brazilian folk and popular music, Milton Nascimento became a key figure in the development of the genre known as "Clube da Esquina." His innovative approach to songwriting and musical arrangements helped broaden the scope of MPB, incorporating elements of jazz, rock, and regional Brazilian music.

These early innovators and pioneers of MPB not only shaped the musical landscape of Brazil but also influenced the global perception of Brazilian music, laying the foundation for the genre's continued growth and evolution. Their artistic contributions continue to resonate within the contemporary music scene, serving as a source of inspiration for generations of musicians and audiences alike.

III. Impact of Jazz, Rock, and Other International Influences

The evolution of Música Popular Brasileira (MPB) has been significantly influenced by a variety of international musical genres, with jazz and rock playing particularly noteworthy roles in shaping the sound and direction of MPB. These international influences have contributed to the diversification and enrichment of the MPB genre, leading to a fusion of styles and the emergence of innovative musical expressions. Some of the key impacts of jazz, rock, and other international influences on MPB include:

1. Jazz Influence: Jazz had a profound impact on the harmonic and melodic structures of MPB, leading to the incorporation of complex chord progressions, improvisational elements, and sophisticated musical arrangements. Artists such as Antonio Carlos Jobim and João Gilberto integrated jazz elements into their compositions, resulting in a more refined and intricate sound that transcended traditional Brazilian music boundaries.

2. Rock Fusion: The infusion of rock elements into MPB brought a more dynamic and electrifying energy to the genre. Artists like Caetano Veloso and Gilberto Gil, who were part of the Tropicália movement, experimented with rock instrumentation and rhythms, creating a unique blend of traditional Brazilian music and contemporary rock sensibilities. This fusion contributed to the genre's modernization and its appeal to younger audiences.

3. World Music Collaborations: The exploration of world music influences, such as African rhythms and European folk traditions, expanded the sonic palette of MPB. Artists began incorporating diverse cultural elements into their music, creating a cross-cultural fusion that reflected the global interconnectedness of music. This cross-pollination not only enriched the rhythmic and melodic aspects of MPB but also fostered a deeper appreciation for cultural diversity within the genre.

4. Fusion with Latin and Caribbean Music: MPB also drew inspiration from Latin American and Caribbean musical traditions, integrating elements such as salsa, reggae, and traditional Cuban music. This fusion contributed to the rhythmic diversity and vivacity of MPB, infusing it with infectious grooves and vibrant melodies that resonated with audiences both in Brazil and internationally.

By assimilating these international influences, MPB expanded its artistic horizons, creating a musical landscape that was both culturally rich and globally resonant. This fusion of diverse musical styles not only revitalized the genre but also contributed to its enduring appeal and relevance within the broader context of global music.

IV. MPB Icons and Legends

Cultural icons have played a pivotal role in shaping the trajectory of Música Popular Brasileira (MPB), both as influential figures within the music industry and as representatives of Brazilian cultural identity. Their artistic contributions and socio-cultural impact have left a lasting imprint on the development and evolution of the genre. Here is a deeper exploration of some key cultural icons and their significant influence on MPB:

1. Chico Buarque: Renowned for his poetic lyrics and evocative storytelling, Chico Buarque is considered one of the most influential figures in the history of MPB. His socially conscious compositions, marked by themes of love, politics, and societal struggles, have contributed to the genre's lyrical depth and emotional resonance. Buarque's distinctive style and lyrical prowess have set a high standard for craftsmanship within MPB, inspiring generations of musicians to embrace introspective storytelling and poetic expression.

2. Elis Regina: Known for her powerful and emotive vocal delivery, Elis Regina remains a beloved figure in the history of Brazilian music. Her interpretive skills and emotional depth allowed her to infuse each performance with a raw intensity that captivated audiences. Regina's collaborations with prominent songwriters and her ability to breathe life into diverse musical genres contributed to the expansion of MPB's stylistic boundaries and its broader cultural appeal.

3. Gilberto Gil: A key figure in the Tropicália movement, Gilberto Gil has been instrumental in bridging the gap between traditional Brazilian music and contemporary global influences. His innovative approach to music, which blended elements of rock, reggae, and African rhythms with MPB, opened up new avenues for artistic exploration within the genre. Gil's commitment to cultural diversity and social activism has reinforced the role of MPB as a platform for social commentary and cultural exchange.

4. Caetano Veloso: Like Gilberto Gil, Caetano Veloso played a central role in the Tropicália movement, advocating for artistic freedom and cultural experimentation. His eclectic musical style, characterized by its fusion of rock, bossa nova, and psychedelic elements, challenged conventional norms and expanded the creative boundaries of MPB. Veloso's intellectualism and artistic innovation have contributed to the genre's progressive spirit, encouraging musicians to embrace a more eclectic and interdisciplinary approach to music-making.

5. Gal Costa: Gal Costa's rich and versatile voice, coupled with her diverse musical repertoire, has made her an influential figure in the world of MPB. Her collaborations with renowned songwriters and her exploration of various musical styles, ranging from bossa nova to psychedelic rock, have contributed to the genre's evolving sound and its ability to adapt to changing musical trends. Costa's contributions have underscored the genre's versatility and its capacity for embracing diverse artistic expressions.

These cultural icons have not only left an indelible mark on the development of MPB but have also contributed to the genre's enduring legacy as a dynamic and influential force within the Brazilian cultural landscape and beyond. Their artistic vision, creative innovation, and commitment to social consciousness continue to inspire contemporary musicians and audiences, ensuring the continued vitality and relevance of MPB in the global music arena.

V. MPB Trailblazers

Trailblazers in the realm of Música Popular Brasileira (MPB) have significantly contributed to the genre's evolution, pushing its creative boundaries and shaping its distinct identity within the broader spectrum of Brazilian music. These visionary artists have introduced innovative approaches to composition, performance, and cultural expression, leaving an enduring legacy that continues to inspire contemporary musicians. Here are some prominent trailblazers and their notable contributions to the MPB genre:

1. Maria Bethânia: Recognized for her powerful and emotionally charged performances, Maria Bethânia has been a trailblazer in the world of MPB. Her rich, deep voice and her ability to convey intense emotions through music have solidified her status as one of Brazil's most revered vocalists. Bethânia's exploration of diverse musical styles, including traditional folk and contemporary trends, has contributed to the genre's dynamic evolution and its ability to resonate with a wide range of audiences.

2. Tom Zé: A pioneering figure within the Tropicália movement, Tom Zé is known for his experimental and avant-garde approach to music. His innovative use of unconventional instruments, electronic sounds, and abstract musical structures has challenged traditional notions of songwriting and performance within MPB. Zé's boundary-pushing musical experiments have expanded the genre's artistic landscape, fostering a spirit of creativity and exploration among subsequent generations of musicians.

3. Nara Leão: Regarded as a key figure in the early development of Bossa Nova, Nara Leão played a vital role in popularizing the genre both in Brazil and internationally. Her collaboration with renowned composers and her dedication to promoting emerging songwriters have contributed to the genre's growth and its capacity for nurturing new talent. Leão's commitment to artistic integrity and her contributions to the preservation of Brazilian musical heritage have cemented her legacy as a trailblazer in the world of MPB.

4. Jorge Ben Jor: A seminal figure in the fusion of traditional Brazilian music with funk and rock elements, Jorge Ben Jor has revolutionized the sound of MPB. His incorporation of Afro-Brazilian rhythms, catchy melodies, and socially conscious lyrics has propelled the genre into new musical territories, fostering a sense of cultural inclusivity and musical innovation. Ben Jor's infectious grooves and dynamic musical arrangements have contributed to the genre's widespread appeal and its ability to transcend cultural and geographical boundaries.

These trailblazers have not only reshaped the sonic landscape of MPB but have also contributed to its cultural significance and global resonance. Their bold artistic visions and pioneering spirit have paved the way for a diverse and dynamic MPB scene, ensuring its continued relevance and influence within the broader context of Brazilian music and the global music industry.

V. Select MPB Artist Legacies

1. Gilberto Gil:

- **Education and Training:** Gilberto Gil was born in Salvador, Bahia, Brazil, and displayed an early affinity for music. He studied business administration at the Federal University of Bahia before fully committing to a musical career.

- **Influences and Innovation:** Influenced by the rich Afro-Brazilian musical traditions of his native Bahia, as well as by global sounds, including rock, reggae, and African music, Gil introduced a diverse array of rhythms and melodies into MPB. His fusion of traditional Brazilian styles with international influences not only expanded the sonic palette of MPB but also contributed to a more inclusive and multicultural approach to Brazilian music.

- **Legacy and Lessons for Musicians:** Gil's fearless experimentation and fusion of diverse musical styles exemplify the importance of embracing cultural diversity and promoting unity through music. His commitment to social activism and cultural exchange serves as a powerful reminder for aspiring musicians to use their art as a platform for advocating social change and fostering cultural understanding.

2. Caetano Veloso:
- **Education and Training:** Caetano Veloso was born in Santo Amaro, Bahia, Brazil, and began his musical career in the vibrant cultural scene of Bahia. He later moved to Rio de Janeiro, where he became a central figure in the Tropicália movement.

- **Influences and Innovation:** Veloso drew inspiration from various sources, including bossa nova, rock, and avant-garde art. His incorporation of experimental and interdisciplinary elements into MPB challenged traditional norms, fostering a more eclectic and progressive approach to Brazilian music.
- **Legacy and Lessons for Musicians:** Veloso's emphasis on artistic freedom and creative exploration serves as a valuable lesson for up-and-coming musicians, encouraging them to push the boundaries of traditional genres and embrace a spirit of artistic experimentation. His intellectual depth and commitment to cultural dialogue underscore the importance of using music as a medium for cultural exchange and social discourse.

3. Milton Nascimento:

- **Education and Training:** Milton Nascimento was born in Rio de Janeiro, Brazil, and was deeply influenced by Brazilian folk music and American jazz. He began his career in the early 1960s and quickly gained recognition for his unique musical style.

- **Influences and Innovation:** Nascimento's incorporation of jazz harmonies and Brazilian folk melodies created a distinctive sound that transcended traditional genres. His use of complex harmonies and rich melodies helped redefine the boundaries of MPB, fostering a more sophisticated and introspective approach to songwriting and musical composition.

- **Legacy and Lessons for Musicians:** Nascimento's ability to seamlessly blend diverse musical influences demonstrates the importance of embracing cultural heritage and fostering a deep appreciation for musical diversity. His emotive storytelling and musical virtuosity serve as an inspiration for aspiring musicians to infuse their work with genuine emotion and artistic integrity.

4. Elis Regina:

- **Education and Training:** Elis Regina was born in Porto Alegre, Brazil, and began her musical career at a young age, winning numerous singing contests. Her powerful and emotive voice quickly garnered attention within the Brazilian music scene.

- **Influences and Innovation:** Regina's dynamic vocal delivery and versatile musical repertoire allowed her to experiment with various genres, including bossa nova, samba, and jazz. Her ability to infuse each performance with raw emotion and intensity redefined the role of the vocalist in MPB, setting a high standard for vocal artistry and emotional expression.

- **Legacy and Lessons for Musicians:** Regina's dedication to musical excellence and her commitment to conveying genuine emotion through her performances serve as a valuable lesson for aspiring musicians. Her ability to connect with audiences on a profound emotional level underscores the importance of developing a strong emotional connection to one's music and audience.

Studying the innovative approaches and enduring legacies of these influential MPB artists can inspire up-and-coming musicians to embrace diversity, experiment with various musical styles, and use their art as a powerful tool for cultural exchange, social commentary, and emotional expression.

VI. Emerging MPB Artists

In recent years, Música Popular Brasileira (MPB) has continued to evolve, embracing modern adaptations, global influences, and innovative collaborations that have expanded its reach and impact both within Brazil and on the international stage. Here is a closer examination of contemporary trends and the global impact of MPB:

Modern Adaptations and Experimentations within MPB:
Contemporary MPB artists have been actively reinterpreting traditional elements of the genre, infusing it with modern production techniques, electronic instrumentation, and diverse

musical influences. These adaptations have resulted in a more eclectic and experimental sound, attracting younger audiences and fostering a renewed interest in the genre. Artists are exploring new sonic territories, blending MPB with genres such as electronic music, indie pop, and hip-hop, creating a fresh and dynamic musical landscape that resonates with contemporary sensibilities.

International Reach and Influence of MPB:

MPB's influence has transcended national borders, gaining recognition and appreciation on the global stage. Its unique blend of Brazilian rhythms, rich melodies, and poetic lyricism has garnered international acclaim, attracting a diverse fan base and fostering cross-cultural dialogue. MPB artists have performed at prominent international music festivals, collaborated with renowned global musicians, and contributed to the enrichment of the global music scene, showcasing the cultural richness and musical diversity of Brazil to audiences worldwide.

Collaboration and Fusion with Global Music Trends:

MPB has embraced collaboration and fusion with a wide array of global music trends, incorporating elements from various genres such as jazz, funk, world music, and contemporary pop. By collaborating with international artists and integrating global musical influences, contemporary MPB musicians have expanded their artistic horizons and contributed to the cross-pollination of musical styles and cultural exchange. This fusion has not only enhanced the sonic depth and diversity of MPB but has also facilitated a deeper appreciation for Brazilian music within the broader context of global music culture.

Through these contemporary trends and its global impact, MPB continues to demonstrate its resilience and relevance in the ever-evolving landscape of world music, serving as a vibrant cultural ambassador for Brazil and a source of inspiration for musicians and music enthusiasts worldwide.

§

Ten Contemporary Música Popular Brasileira (MPB) Artists of Note:

1. Céu:
- **Bio:** Céu is known for her fusion of bossa nova, samba, and electronic elements, creating a unique sound that transcends traditional genres.
- **Notable Recording:** "Céu" (2005)
- **Label:** Six Degrees Records

2. Marisa Monte:
- **Bio:** Marisa Monte is celebrated for her versatile vocal style and her ability to blend MPB with diverse musical influences, including pop and rock.
- **Notable Recording:** "Memórias, Crônicas e Declarações de Amor" (2000)
- **Label:** EMI

3. Seu Jorge:
- **Bio:** Seu Jorge is renowned for his soulful voice and his modern take on samba, combining traditional Brazilian sounds with contemporary elements.
- **Notable Recording:** "Cru" (2005)
- **Label:** Wrasse Records

4. Maria Gadú:
- **Bio:** Maria Gadú is known for her intimate and heartfelt compositions that blend elements of MPB with pop and acoustic folk influences.
- **Notable Recording:** "Maria Gadú" (2009)
- **Label:** Universal Music

5. Lenine:
- **Bio:** Lenine is recognized for his socially conscious lyrics and his innovative fusion of MPB with Afro-Brazilian rhythms and rock influences.
- **Notable Recording:** "O Dia em Que Faremos Contato" (2003)
- **Label:** Universal Music

6. Mallu Magalhães:
- **Bio:** Mallu Magalhães is known for her folk-inspired melodies and introspective songwriting that have earned her a prominent place within the contemporary MPB scene.
- **Notable Recording:** "Mallu Magalhães" (2008)
- **Label:** Sony Music

7. Silva:
- **Bio:** Silva is celebrated for his innovative blend of traditional Brazilian sounds with modern electronic music, creating a fresh and captivating musical experience.
- **Notable Recording:** "Silva Canta Marisa" (2016)
- **Label:** Som Livre

8. Roberta Sá:
- **Bio:** Roberta Sá is known for her soulful voice and her exploration of diverse Brazilian rhythms, infusing her music with elements of samba, bossa nova, and MPB.
- **Notable Recording:** "Braseiro" (2012)
- **Label:** Deckdisc

9. Emicida:
- **Bio:** Emicida is recognized for his socially conscious rap lyrics and his contributions to the fusion of hip-hop with Brazilian musical traditions, reflecting the contemporary urban culture of Brazil.
- **Notable Recording:** "O Glorioso Retorno de Quem Nunca Esteve Aqui" (2013)
- **Label:** Laboratório Fantasma

10. Liniker:
- **Bio:** Liniker is celebrated for their soulful voice and their bold, genre-defying approach to music, which combines elements of MPB, soul, and R&B, while exploring themes of identity and self-acceptance.
- **Notable Recording:** "Remonta" (2016)
- **Label:** RISCO.

The new wave of Música Popular Brasileira (MPB) continues to be shaped by a vibrant array of emerging artists who are making unique and innovative contributions to the genre. These artists are exploring diverse sounds and styles, leveraging technology and digital platforms to reach wider audiences and redefine the landscape of contemporary Brazilian music. Here is a closer look at the new wave of MPB:

Emerging Artists and Their Unique Contributions:
A new generation of MPB artists, including names such as Duda Beat, Xênia França, and Josyara, are making their mark with fresh perspectives and innovative musical approaches. Duda Beat is known for her fusion of pop and electronic elements with traditional MPB, creating a distinctive and danceable sound. Xênia França explores Afro-Brazilian rhythms and soulful melodies, infusing her music with a powerful blend of social commentary and cultural heritage. Josyara experiments with folk-inspired sounds and intimate storytelling, offering a contemporary take on traditional Brazilian music.

Exploration of Innovative Sounds and Styles:
Contemporary MPB artists are delving into an array of innovative sounds and styles, blending traditional Brazilian music with global influences such as indie rock, electronic music, and R&B. They are reinterpreting classic MPB elements with a modern sensibility, incorporating experimental production techniques and unconventional musical arrangements. This exploration has led to the creation of a dynamic and eclectic MPB landscape that appeals to a diverse and contemporary audience.

Impact of Technology and Digital Platforms on the Genre:
The rise of technology and digital platforms has provided new avenues for MPB artists to connect with audiences worldwide. Artists are leveraging social media, streaming platforms, and digital marketing tools to promote their music, build fan communities, and engage with a global fan base. The accessibility of digital distribution has facilitated the exposure of MPB to a broader international audience, enabling emerging artists to gain recognition and establish their presence in the global music industry.

Through their innovative contributions, exploration of diverse sounds, and utilization of digital platforms, the new wave of

MPB artists is redefining the genre, shaping its contemporary identity, and ensuring its continued relevance within the dynamic landscape of Brazilian and global music.

§

Cross-cultural exchange and collaboration have played a pivotal role in the evolution of Música Popular Brasileira (MPB), fostering a rich and dynamic musical dialogue between Brazil and the global music community. The genre's reception and influence in different global contexts have contributed to its international acclaim, while also presenting unique challenges and opportunities within a globalized world. Here is an exploration of these dynamics:

Cross-Cultural Exchange and Collaboration in MPB:
MPB has been instrumental in facilitating cross-cultural exchange and collaboration, serving as a bridge between Brazilian musical traditions and global genres. Through collaborations with international artists, MPB musicians have integrated diverse cultural influences, enriching their sound and broadening their global appeal. This cross-cultural exchange has not only deepened mutual artistic understanding but has also fostered a sense of cultural unity and shared creativity across borders.

Reception and Influence of MPB in Different Global Contexts:
MPB's distinctive blend of Brazilian rhythms, poetic lyricism, and cultural diversity has garnered significant appreciation and influence in various global contexts. Its melodic richness and emotional depth have resonated with audiences worldwide, leading to the incorporation of MPB elements into diverse musical genres and cultural expressions. The genre's influence can be seen in the works of international artists who have drawn inspiration from its rhythmic intricacies and social commentary, thereby contributing to the genre's global legacy and continued relevance.

Challenges and Opportunities for MPB in a Globalized World:
While the globalized world has provided MPB with opportunities for international recognition and cultural exchange, it has also presented challenges such as preserving its authentic cultural identity amidst commercialization and homogenization. Additionally, language barriers and cultural nuances may pose

obstacles to the widespread dissemination of MPB in certain global markets. However, the digital age has offered new platforms for promoting MPB globally, allowing artists to connect with diverse audiences and cultivate a dedicated fan base beyond national boundaries.

By embracing cross-cultural exchange, navigating global reception and influence, and addressing the challenges and opportunities of a globalized world, MPB continues to solidify its position as a cultural ambassador, fostering mutual understanding, and celebrating the rich tapestry of global musical heritage.

119

Chapter 6. Introduction to Brazilian Jazz

Brazilian Jazz is a musical genre that emerges from the rich tapestry of Brazil's cultural heritage and the improvisational spirit of jazz. With its roots deeply intertwined in the diverse traditions of Brazil, this genre represents a harmonious fusion of African rhythms, European harmonies, and indigenous musical expressions, all seamlessly interwoven with the improvisational language of jazz. The evolution of Brazilian Jazz is a testament to the cultural vitality and artistic ingenuity that have flourished within the vibrant musical landscape of Brazil.

Origins and Historical Evolution

The roots of Brazilian Jazz can be traced back to the early 20th century, when a wave of cultural exchange and musical experimentation swept through Brazil. Influenced by traditional Brazilian music forms such as samba, choro, and bossa nova, as well as by the innovative sounds of American jazz, Brazilian musicians began to infuse their compositions with a unique blend of rhythmic intricacies, melodic richness, and improvisational techniques, giving birth to a distinctive Brazilian interpretation of jazz.

Cultural Significance and Influences

Brazilian Jazz holds profound cultural significance, serving as a powerful medium for cultural expression, social commentary, and the preservation of Brazil's musical heritage. Its diverse influences reflect the multicultural fabric of Brazilian society, incorporating elements from African, European, and indigenous traditions, as well as the dynamic energy of urban life. This genre not only embodies the collective memory of Brazil's complex cultural narrative but also serves as a vehicle for cultural exchange and cross-pollination between Brazil and the global jazz community.

As we delve into the intricate world of Brazilian Jazz, it becomes evident that its evolution and cultural significance are deeply rooted in the multifaceted history and diverse cultural traditions of Brazil, embodying the spirit of artistic innovation, cultural resilience, and the transformative power of musical expression.

I. Key Musical Elements in Brazilian Jazz

Rhythmic Patterns and Percussion:
In Brazilian Jazz, rhythmic patterns and percussion play a
fundamental role, drawing inspiration from the rich tradition of
Afro-Brazilian rhythms. The incorporation of syncopated beats,
polyrhythms, and intricate percussion arrangements reflects the
influence of traditional Brazilian music genres such as samba,
bossa nova, and maracatu. These rhythmic complexities create
a dynamic and infectious groove that serves as the heartbeat of
Brazilian Jazz, infusing the music with an irresistible sense of
energy and movement.

Melodic Structures and Harmonies:
Melodic structures and harmonies in Brazilian Jazz are
characterized by their vibrant and colorful tonal palette, reflecting
the diverse cultural influences that have shaped the genre.
The use of extended chords, modal scales, and rich harmonic
textures demonstrates the fusion of traditional Brazilian melodic
sensibilities with the sophisticated harmonies of jazz. This unique
blend of melodic structures and harmonies allows Brazilian Jazz
to evoke a sense of emotional depth and musical sophistication,
creating a harmonious balance between complexity and lyrical
expression.

Improvisation Techniques:
Improvisation lies at the heart of Brazilian Jazz, serving as a
dynamic and expressive form of musical storytelling. Drawing
from the improvisational traditions of jazz and the spontaneous
spirit of Brazilian music, musicians engage in intricate
melodic improvisations, rhythmic variations, and call-and-
response exchanges, creating a dialogue between instruments
and performers. The art of improvisation in Brazilian Jazz is
characterized by its fluidity, inventiveness, and the seamless
integration of diverse musical elements, allowing musicians to
explore and interpret the musical landscape with spontaneity and
creativity.

Understanding these key musical elements in Brazilian Jazz is
essential for appreciating the genre's unique rhythmic vitality,
melodic richness, and improvisational fervor, all of which
contribute to the genre's enduring appeal and artistic innovation.

II. Experimentation in Brazilian Jazz

Brazilian jazz is particularly notable for its propensity towards experimentation, incorporation of unique instrumentation, exploration of unconventional time signatures, and innovative orchestration. While traditional Brazilian jazz encompasses elements of samba, bossa nova, and other native styles, it has also demonstrated a willingness to incorporate "out" jazz elements and avantgarde tendencies.

Experimentation in Brazilian jazz often manifests in the blending of traditional Brazilian rhythms with contemporary jazz improvisation techniques, resulting in a fusion of diverse musical vocabularies. This fusion allows for the exploration of unconventional time signatures, offering a departure from standard rhythmic structures and providing a platform for rhythmic complexity and innovation.

Moreover, Brazilian jazz has been known to feature unusual instrumentation, incorporating indigenous and folk instruments alongside traditional jazz ensembles. This incorporation of diverse instruments contributes to the unique sonic palette of Brazilian jazz, adding layers of texture and cultural depth to the music.

In terms of orchestration, Brazilian jazz frequently experiments with unconventional arrangements, showcasing a willingness to challenge traditional orchestral norms. This approach often results in dynamic and eclectic soundscapes, characterized by intricate layering and a rich blend of timbres, reflecting the genre's propensity for sonic exploration and creative expression.

Additionally, Brazilian jazz groups may vary in size, ranging from small ensembles to larger orchestral arrangements. This flexibility in group size allows for the exploration of different musical dynamics and interactions, contributing to the genre's versatility and adaptability to various performance settings and contexts.

The spirit of experimentation, the use of unconventional instrumentation, and the exploration of odd time signatures and orchestration all contribute to the distinctive and innovative nature of Brazilian jazz, solidifying its position as a dynamic and evolving genre within the broader landscape of jazz music.

How is this done, precisely?

Here are some examples of experimental orchestrations, arrangements, instruments, and rhythmic patterns that have been utilized in the realm of Brazilian jazz, showcasing the genre's innovative and dynamic musical landscape:

Experimental Orchestrations and Arrangements:

1. Arranging Brazilian folk melodies for a jazz big band, incorporating complex harmonic structures and intricate rhythmic arrangements.

2. Fusing traditional samba rhythms with contemporary brass arrangements, showcasing a dynamic blend of brass instrumentation and percussive elements.

3. Experimenting with unconventional ensemble configurations, such as combining string quartets with traditional Brazilian percussion instruments, creating a unique sonic fusion of classical and Brazilian jazz elements.

Innovative Instrumentation:

1. Incorporating Brazilian folk instruments, such as the berimbau, cuica, and pandeiro, within a jazz ensemble to add layers of indigenous Brazilian sounds and textures.

2. Integrating electronic instruments, such as synthesizers and samplers, with traditional Brazilian percussion and wind instruments to create a modern fusion of electronic and acoustic elements.

3. Exploring the use of nontraditional jazz instruments, including the cavaquinho, bandolim, and accordion, to add a distinctive and folkinspired tonal quality to the overall ensemble sound.

Rhythmic Patterns and Textures:

1. Experimenting with complex poly-rhythmic structures, combining traditional Brazilian rhythmic patterns, such as baião and maracatu, with intricate jazz syncopations and cross-rhythms.

2. Incorporating irregular and asymmetric time signatures, such as 7/8 and 9/8, within the framework of traditional jazz compositions, creating a sense of rhythmic tension and complexity.

3. Integrating call-and-response rhythmic motifs between different sections of the ensemble, highlighting the interplay between various instrumental voices and contributing to the dynamic and interactive nature of the music.

These examples illustrate the innovative and boundary-pushing nature of Brazilian jazz, emphasizing the genre's willingness to experiment with diverse musical elements and techniques to create a rich and dynamic musical tapestry that reflects the cultural diversity and artistic vitality of Brazil.

III. Notable Brazilian Jazz Artists and Their Contributions

1. João Gilberto:
Bio: Known as a pioneer of bossa nova, João Gilberto was a Brazilian singer and guitarist, recognized for his soft singing style and innovative guitar playing.
Significant Recording: "Chega de Saudade" (1959)
Label: Odeon
Dates: 1931-2019
Influences: Traditional Brazilian music, jazz harmonies
Legacy: Helped popularize bossa nova globally, influencing generations of musicians.

2. Antonio Carlos Jobim:
Bio: Renowned as one of the most important figures in bossa nova, Jobim was a Brazilian composer, pianist, and songwriter, celebrated for his sophisticated melodies and harmonies.
Significant Recording: "The Composer of Desafinado Plays" (1963)
Label: Verve Records
Dates: 1927-1994
Influences: Brazilian samba, American jazz
Legacy: Widely regarded as one of the greatest

songwriters of the 20th century, his compositions remain jazz standards.

3. Hermeto Pascoal:

Bio: A virtuoso multi-instrumentalist and composer, Pascoal is known for his avant-garde approach to jazz, incorporating Brazilian folk elements and experimental sounds.
Significant Recording: "Slaves Mass" (1977)
Label: Warner Bros. Records
Dates: Born in 1936
Influences: Brazilian folk music, jazz improvisation
Legacy: Pioneered a unique blend of Brazilian folk and jazz, known for his fearless musical experimentation.

4. Baden Powell:

Bio: Baden Powell de Aquino was a Brazilian guitarist and composer known for his innovative approach that blended classical techniques with Brazilian rhythms, contributing significantly to bossa nova and Brazilian jazz.
Significant Recording: "Tristeza on Guitar" (1966)
Label: MPS Records, Barclay
Dates: 1937-2000
Influences: Brazilian choro, samba, and jazz
Legacy: Revered for his virtuosic guitar skills and musical fusion, he expanded the possibilities of Brazilian guitar music on the global stage.

5. Egberto Gismonti:

Bio: Egberto Gismonti is a Brazilian multi instrumentalist, composer, and arranger renowned for his groundbreaking work that incorporates elements of traditional Brazilian music, jazz, and classical music, creating a distinctive and eclectic musical style.
Significant Recording: "Dança das Cabeças" (1977)
Label: ECM Records
Dates: Born in 1947
Influences: Brazilian folk music, classical music, and jazz
Legacy: Known for his exceptional virtuosity and genre-bending compositions, he has played a pivotal role in the evolution of contemporary Brazilian instrumental music.

6. Joyce:

Bio: Joyce Moreno, known simply as Joyce, is a Brazilian singersongwriter and guitarist celebrated for her contributions to the MPB genre, fusing traditional Brazilian music with elements of jazz, bossa nova, and rock.

Significant Recording: "Feminina" (1980)

Label: Odeon, Far Out Recordings

Dates: Born in 1948

Influences: Bossa nova, samba, and Brazilian popular music

Legacy: Recognized for her rich, velvety vocals and poetic songwriting, she has been an influential figure in the development of modern Brazilian music, inspiring a generation of musicians.

7.Moacir Santos:

Bio: Moacir Santos was a Brazilian multi-instrumentalist, composer, and music educator known for his significant contributions to Brazilian jazz and his innovative orchestral arrangements that combined elements of Brazilian music with modern jazz.

Significant Recording: "Coisas" (1965)

Label: Forma, Blue Note

Dates: 1926-2006

Influences: Brazilian folk music, jazz, and classical music

Legacy: Revered for his complex compositions and arrangements, he played a crucial role in shaping the sound of modern Brazilian jazz.

8. Dom Um Romão:

Bio: Dom Um Romão was a Brazilian jazz drummer and percussionist celebrated for his unique rhythmic sensibilities and his versatile contributions to the world of jazz, showcasing a fusion of Brazilian rhythms with contemporary jazz elements.

Significant Recording: "Dom Um" (1973)

Label: Muse Records, Pablo Records

Dates: 1925-2005

Influences: Brazilian samba, jazz, and Latin music

Legacy: Renowned for his exceptional percussion skills and his ability to seamlessly blend diverse musical influences, he left a lasting impact on the global jazz community.

9. Tania Maria:

Bio: Tania Maria is a Brazilian singer, pianist, and composer recognized for her vivacious performances and her unique blend of Brazilian rhythms, jazz, and AfroCuban influences, creating an exuberant and dynamic musical style.
Significant Recording: "Piquant" (1981)
Label: Concord Jazz, Capitol Records
Dates: Born in 1948
Influences: Brazilian bossa nova, jazz, and Latin music
Legacy: Known for her fiery piano playing and infectious vocal delivery, she has made a significant contribution to the fusion of Brazilian music with contemporary jazz and Latin genres.

10. Edison Machado:

Bio: Edison Machado was a Brazilian drummer known for his pioneering contributions to the bossa nova movement and his innovative approach to blending samba rhythms with jazz, contributing to the development of the Brazilian jazz drumming style.
Significant Recording: "É Samba Novo" (1964)
Label: Philips
Dates: 1934-1990
Influences: Brazilian samba, jazz
Legacy: Revered for his rhythmic dexterity and dynamic drumming style, he played a crucial role in popularizing Brazilian rhythms within the context of modern jazz.

11. J.T. Meirelles:

Bio: J.T. Meirelles was a Brazilian saxophonist and arranger recognized for his significant contributions to the Brazilian jazz and bossa nova scenes, renowned for his soulful saxophone playing and his skillful arrangements.
Significant Recording: "O Som" (1966)
Label: Polydor
Dates: 1928-2008
Influences: Jazz, Brazilian popular music
Legacy: Known for his melodic improvisations and vibrant arrangements, he made a lasting impact on the development of the Brazilian jazz sound.

12. Cesar Camargo Mariano:

Bio: Cesar Camargo Mariano is a Brazilian pianist, composer, and arranger known for his versatile contributions to Brazilian jazz, showcasing a fusion of traditional Brazilian rhythms with contemporary jazz harmonies and arrangements.
Significant Recording: "São Paulo Brasil" (1976)
Label: RCA Victor, Columbia
Dates: Born in 1943
Influences: Brazilian music, jazz, and Latin music
Legacy: Celebrated for his sophisticated compositions and his dynamic piano playing, he has been a key figure in the evolution of Brazilian jazz and popular music.

13. Victor Assis Brasil:

Bio: Victor Assis Brasil was a Brazilian saxophonist and composer recognized for his exceptional technical prowess and his innovative approach to blending traditional Brazilian music with elements of modern jazz and postbop.
Significant Recording: "Esperanto" (1965)
Label: Forma, EMIOdeon
Dates: 1945-1981
Influences: Jazz, bossa nova, and Brazilian folk music
Legacy: Regarded for his melodic ingenuity and his contributions to the Brazilian jazz saxophone tradition, he remains an influential figure in the world of Brazilian instrumental music.

14. Claudio Roditi:

Bio: Claudio Roditi was a Brazilian jazz trumpeter and flugelhorn player known for his lyrical playing style and his versatile contributions to the world of jazz, showcasing a fusion of Brazilian musical influences with bebop and hard bop.
Significant Recording: "Milestones" (1995)
Label: Candid, Nagel Heyer
Dates: 1946-2020
Influences: Jazz, Brazilian music, and Latin music
Legacy: Celebrated for his warm tone and expressive improvisations, he has made a significant impact on the development of Latin jazz and Brazilian jazz on the global stage.

15. Flora Purim:

Bio: Flora Purim is a Brazilian jazz singer known for her versatile vocal abilities and her contributions to the fusion of Brazilian music with jazz and Latin jazz, showcasing a dynamic and expressive vocal style.
Significant Recording: "Butterfly Dreams" (1973)
Label: Milestone, Warner Bros. Records
Dates: Born in 1942
Influences: Brazilian samba, jazz, and Latin music
Legacy: Revered for her innovative vocal improvisations and her role in popularizing Brazilian jazz fusion, she remains an influential figure in the world of vocal jazz.

16. Airto Moreira:

Bio: Airto Moreira is a Brazilian percussionist and drummer celebrated for his contributions to the world of jazz and his influential role in popularizing Brazilian rhythms and percussion instruments within the jazz and fusion genres.
Significant Recording: "Fingers" (1973)
Label: CTI Records, Warner Bros. Records
Dates: Born in 1941
Influences: Brazilian folk music, jazz, and Latin music
Legacy: Renowned for his dynamic and expressive percussion work, he has played a crucial role in the development of the jazz fusion movement and the integration of Brazilian rhythms into contemporary jazz music.

17. Laurindo Almeida:

Bio: Laurindo Almeida was a Brazilian guitarist and composer known for his virtuosic guitar playing and his contributions to the integration of Brazilian music with jazz and classical music, showcasing a unique blend of Brazilian and European musical traditions.
Significant Recording: "Concerto de Copacabana" (1953)
Label: Capitol Records, Decca
Dates: 1917-1995
Influences: Brazilian choro, classical music, and jazz
Legacy: Celebrated for his classical guitar interpretations and his collaborations with prominent jazz musicians, he remains an influential figure in the history of Brazilian jazz guitar.

18. Luiz Bonfá:

Bio: Luiz Bonfá was a Brazilian guitarist and composer known for his significant contributions to bossa nova and Brazilian jazz, renowned for his melodic guitar playing and his evocative compositions.
Significant Recording: "Amor! The Fabulous Guitar of Luiz Bonfá" (1964)
Label: Verve Records
Dates: 1922-2001
Influences: Brazilian samba, jazz, and classical music
Legacy: Revered for his expressive and lyrical guitar style, he has left a lasting legacy in the realm of Brazilian jazz and popular music.

19.Sergio Mendes:

Bio: Sérgio Mendes is a Brazilian pianist, composer, and bandleader recognized for his influential contributions to the world of bossa nova and Brazilian jazz, renowned for his vibrant and infectious musical style.
Significant Recording: "Brasil '66" (1966)
Label: A&M Records
Dates: Born in 1941
Influences: Brazilian samba, jazz, and Latin music
Legacy: Celebrated for his successful blend of Brazilian rhythms with pop and jazz, he has been a key figure in popularizing Brazilian music internationally.

20. Astrud Gilberto:

Bio: Astrud Gilberto is a Brazilian singer recognized for her iconic vocal contributions to bossa nova and Brazilian jazz, known for her warm and intimate vocal style that has captivated audiences worldwide.
Significant Recording: "The Astrud Gilberto Album" (1965)
Label: Verve Records
Dates: Born in 1940
Influences: Bossa nova, jazz, and traditional Brazilian music
Legacy: Renowned for her timeless recordings and her role in introducing bossa nova to the international music scene, she remains an influential figure in the history of Brazilian jazz vocals.

21. Nana Vasconcelos:

Bio: Nana Vasconcelos was a Brazilian percussionist and berimbau player known for his innovative and influential contributions to world music, showcasing a fusion of Brazilian rhythmic traditions with a diverse range of global musical styles.
Significant Recording: "Saudades" (1980)
Label: ECM Records
Dates: 1944-2016
Influences: Brazilian percussion, jazz, and world music
Legacy: Celebrated for his virtuosic and expressive percussion performances, he has played a crucial role in expanding the possibilities of percussion in the context of contemporary jazz and global music genres.

Nana Vasconcelos was revered for his mastery of percussion instruments and his ability to infuse traditional Brazilian rhythms with a contemporary and global musical sensibility, leaving behind a rich legacy of innovative and influential contributions to the world of music.

22. Eumir Deodato:

Bio: Eumir Deodato is a Brazilian pianist, composer, and arranger celebrated for his influential contributions to Brazilian jazz and the fusion of traditional Brazilian music with contemporary jazz and funk, showcasing a dynamic and eclectic musical style.
Significant Recording: "Prelude" (1973)
Label: CTI Records
Dates: Born in 1942
Influences: Brazilian bossa nova, jazz, and funk
Legacy: Recognized for his sophisticated compositions and innovative arrangements, he has been a key figure in the evolution of Brazilian jazz and the popularization of jazz fusion, leaving a lasting impact on the global music scene.

Eumir Deodato's versatile musical talents and his ability to seamlessly blend diverse musical influences have solidified his position as an influential figure in the history of Brazilian jazz and the broader landscape of contemporary jazz fusion.

4. Fusion of Brazilian and Jazz Traditions

The fusion of Brazilian and jazz traditions has resulted in a dynamic and rich musical tapestry, blending the rhythmic vibrancy of Brazilian music with the improvisational and harmonic complexity of jazz. This fusion has seen an exploration of various Brazilian musical genres, including samba and Bossa Nova, as well as the integration of Afro-Brazilian rhythms into the jazz idiom.

Exploration of Samba and Bossa Nova Influences:
The incorporation of samba and Bossa Nova influences into jazz has contributed to the development of a vibrant and infectious rhythmic language within the jazz framework. Artists have experimented with the syncopated grooves and melodic subtleties inherent in these Brazilian styles, infusing their compositions with a sense of energy and playfulness while maintaining the sophistication and improvisational spirit of jazz.

Integration of Afro-Brazilian Rhythms in Jazz:
The integration of Afro-Brazilian rhythms into jazz has expanded the rhythmic palette of the genre, adding layers of complexity and depth to the music. Artists have drawn inspiration from the rich heritage of Afro-Brazilian music, incorporating intricate polyrhythmic patterns, pulsating percussion arrangements, and pulsating grooves that create a dynamic and engaging musical experience, enriching the jazz tradition with the vibrant spirit of Brazilian rhythms.

Through the fusion of samba, Bossa Nova, and Afro-Brazilian rhythms with the intricacies of jazz, musicians have cultivated a diverse and innovative musical language that celebrates the cultural richness of Brazil while expanding the boundaries of the jazz genre.

American Artists Influenced by Brazilian Music and Brazilian Jazz

1. Pat Metheny: With his distinctive guitar style and innovative approach to jazz fusion, Pat Metheny has explored Brazilian musical influences in various albums, showcasing a deep appreciation for Brazilian rhythms and harmonies, incorporating them seamlessly into his jazz compositions.

Suggested listening:

"Offramp" (1982): Although not entirely Brazilian-themed, "Are You Going with Me?" on this album is notable for its Brazilian-inspired rhythms and textures.

"Rejoicing" (1984): This album features "Loro," a composition by Egberto Gismonti, a Brazilian multi-instrumentalist. The track exemplifies Metheny's exploration of Brazilian influences in his jazz guitar work.

"Still Life (Talking)" (1987): While not strictly Brazilian, this album is influenced by world music, and tracks like "Last Train Home" incorporate subtle Brazilian rhythmic elements into the jazz framework.

"Letter from Home" (1989): This album features "Beat 70," which has a distinctly Brazilian rhythmic feel and showcases Metheny's exploration of Brazilian musical idioms.

"Secret Story" (1992): This ambitious project by Metheny is heavily influenced by various world music traditions, including Brazilian rhythms and textures, creating a rich tapestry of global musical influences.

Nana Vasconcelos, the Brazilian percussionist, collaborated with Pat Metheny on various occasions, contributing his unique percussion work to the overall sound of the albums.

While these albums may not be solely dedicated to Brazilian music, they represent Metheny's fascination with Brazilian influences and his exploration of the rich musical traditions that Brazil has to offer.

2. Joni Mitchell: Known for her expressive songwriting and versatile musical style, Joni Mitchell has incorporated elements of Brazilian music into her work, drawing from the rhythmic intricacies and melodic sensibilities of the genre to add a unique flair to her folk and jazz-infused compositions.

Suggested listening:

"The Hissing of Summer Lawns" (1975): This album features elements of jazz and world music, with tracks such as "The Jungle Line" incorporating rhythmic patterns and instrumentation inspired by Brazilian music, reflecting Mitchell's experimental approach to blending diverse musical styles.

"Don Juan's Reckless Daughter" (1977): In this album, Mitchell's experimental inclinations become apparent, and while the influences are diverse, there are hints of Brazilian rhythmic sensibilities, showcasing her interest in incorporating global musical elements into her compositions.

3. Michael Franks: Michael Franks' smooth jazz and pop compositions often incorporate Brazilian musical elements, such as Bossa Nova-inspired rhythms and lush harmonies, creating a signature sound that blends elements of Brazilian music with contemporary jazz and pop sensibilities.

Suggested listening

1. "The Lady Wants to Know" from the album "Sleeping Gypsy" (1977, Warner Bros. Records) - This track exemplifies Franks' seamless incorporation of Bossa Nova elements, featuring smooth jazz textures and alluring rhythmic patterns that evoke the essence of Brazilian musical traditions.

2. "Popsicle Toes" from the album "The Art of Tea" (1975, Reprise Records) - Reflecting Franks' penchant for incorporating breezy melodies and mellow harmonies, this song combines elements of Bossa Nova with his signature jazz-pop sensibilities, creating a laid-back and inviting musical atmosphere.

3. "Antonio's Song (The Rainbow)" from the album "Burchfield Nines" (1978, Warner Bros. Records) - This track highlights Franks' tribute to the influential

Brazilian musician Antonio Carlos
Jobim, known for his pivotal role in popularizing
Bossa Nova. The song resonates with Jobim's
melodic and harmonic language, demonstrating
Franks' admiration for Brazilian musical
traditions.

Through his exploration of Brazilian musical styles and tropes,
Michael Franks has crafted a unique and sophisticated sound that
combines the smoothness of jazz with the rhythmic intricacies
of Bossa Nova, showcasing a musical journey that celebrates the
cross-cultural exchange between American jazz and Brazilian
music.

Finally, in older performance videos, Franks is seen playing what
appears to be an instrument found in Brazil called the xequerê or
shekere.

The xequerê is originally from West Africa and is a staple of
African and Afro-Brazilian music. It consists of a gourd (cabaça)
cut in the middle and then wrapped in a net in which beads
or small plastic balls are threaded. The instrument is shaken
to produce its musical noise. The afoxé is a similar, smaller
instrument. The shekere is also found in Brazil and is a larger
version of the xequerê. It is a Yoruba percussion instrument
consisting of a dried gourd with beads or cowries woven into a net
covering the gourd. The shekere is common in West African and
Latin American folkloric traditions as well as some of the popular
music styles. In performance, it is shaken and/or hit against
the hands. The shape of the gourd determines the sound of the
instrument. The bigger the gourd is, the louder the sound as more
beads have a space to move around.

**4. Paul Simon's "Rhythm of the Saints" (October 16, 1990,
Warner Bros. Records).** Paul Simon's album "Rhythm of the
Saints" draws heavily from Brazilian musical traditions, featuring
intricate percussion arrangements, rich polyrhythmic textures,
and the incorporation of Afro-Brazilian influences, creating a
compelling fusion of Brazilian rhythms with Simon's distinct
songwriting style. While the album is generally well-remembered
as a creative fusion or a unique exploration of Brazilian and
global musical influences and evidently was at least a partial
collaboration with authentic Brazilian musicians, time and

distance makes some of it come across as a somewhat forced follow-up to the significantly more inspired, African-influenced 'Graceland'. Nevertheless, Suggested listening:

1. The Obvious Child: This track incorporates Brazilian percussion elements, including the use of surdo drums, which contribute to the vibrant rhythmic texture and energy of the song.

2. Can't Run But: Brazilian rhythmic influences are evident in the intricate percussion arrangements, reflecting the pulsating energy and dynamic syncopation characteristic of Afro-Brazilian music.

3. The Coast: Drawing from Brazilian musical traditions, this track infuses elements of samba and Bossa Nova, creating a rich rhythmic backdrop that complements the introspective lyrical theme of the song.

4. Proof: "Proof" features polyrhythmic textures and intricate percussion patterns inspired by Brazilian musical styles, adding a layer of complexity and depth to the song's overall sonic landscape.

5. Further to Fly: Brazilian rhythmic sensibilities are subtly interwoven into the composition, enriching the melodic framework and contributing to the song's emotional depth and expressive nuances.

6. She Moves On: This track embraces Brazilian influences through its rhythmic complexity and percussion arrangements, creating a dynamic and captivating sonic experience that reflects Simon's exploration of global musical traditions.

7. Born at the Right Time: While not as explicitly Brazilian-influenced as some other tracks, "Born at the Right Time" still incorporates subtle rhythmic elements and melodic nuances that nod to Simon's broader exploration of world music traditions.

For some, "Rhythm of the Saints" shows Paul Simon skillfully integrating Brazilian musical influences, showcasing a deep appreciation for the rhythmic intricacies and melodic richness of Brazilian music, and contributing to the album's rich and diverse sonic tapestry.

A list of Brazilian artists who contributed to the album:
- Naná Vasconcelos: percussion
- Jorjão Barreto: keyboards
- Armando Marçal: percussion
- Dom Chacal: percussion
- Mingo Araújo: percussion
- Cyro Baptista: percussion
- Olodum: percussion
- Grupo Cultural Olodum: percussion

5. Charlie Byrd: Charlie Byrd's exploration of Brazilian music, particularly Bossa Nova, helped introduce the genre to a wider American audience, showcasing the beautiful interplay between Brazilian rhythms and jazz harmonies.

Suggested listening

1. "Desafinado" (1962): Byrd's rendition of this Antonio Carlos Jobim classic highlights his masterful interpretation of Brazilian Bossa Nova, incorporating the genre's signature rhythmic patterns and melodic sensibilities into his guitar playing.

2. "Bamba Samba" (1962): This album features Byrd's original composition "Bamba Samba," which blends elements of samba and Bossa Nova, showcasing his adeptness at infusing Brazilian rhythmic nuances into his jazz guitar arrangements.

3. "Brazilian Byrd" (1965): This album serves as a testament to Byrd's deep appreciation for Brazilian music, featuring a collection of Brazilian-inspired compositions that reflect the vibrant spirit and rich musical heritage of Brazil.

Charlie Byrd's recordings demonstrate his profound affinity for Brazilian music, with his masterful guitar work capturing the essence of Bossa Nova and other Brazilian musical styles, ultimately contributing to the popularization of Brazilian music in the United States and beyond.

6. Herbie Mann: With his penchant for musical exploration, Herbie Mann incorporated Brazilian influences into his jazz repertoire, experimenting with various Brazilian styles and contributing to the popularization of Brazilian music in the United States.

Suggested listening

"Do the Bossa Nova with Herbie Mann" (1962): This album features Mann's early exploration of Brazilian music and includes covers of Brazilian standards like "Desafinado" and "One Note Samba."

"Brazil, Bossa Nova & Blues" (1962): This album features Mann's fusion of Brazilian music with blues and jazz. It includes covers of Brazilian standards like "Manhã de Carnaval" and "Insensatez."

"Herbie Mann Live at Newport" (1963): This live album features Mann's performance at the Newport Jazz Festival and includes his popular cover of "Comin' Home Baby" as well as a version of "Caravan" with Brazilian percussion.

"The Inspiration I Feel" (1968): This album features Mann's exploration of Brazilian music and includes covers of Brazilian standards like "A Felicidade" and "Triste."

"Brazil: Once Again" (1978): This album marks Mann's return to the Brazilian influences that first emerged on his early 1960s albums. It includes covers of Brazilian standards like "Lugar Comum" and "O Meu Amor Chorou."

7. Duke Ellington: Duke Ellington's musical experiments often included forays into world music, including Brazilian influences, showcasing his innovative arrangements and compositions that seamlessly blended elements of Brazilian music with his distinctive jazz orchestration.

Suggested listening

"Carnaval Jungle" (1966): This piece, inspired by the energy and vibrancy of Brazilian carnivals, features dynamic rhythms and orchestration that evoke the spirit of Brazilian music, showcasing Ellington's ability to infuse diverse musical traditions into his compositions.

"Moonbow" (1966): While not strictly Brazilian, this composition incorporates rhythmic elements that nod to the lively and pulsating rhythms often found in Brazilian music, displaying Ellington's creative exploration of global musical styles.

"Chico Cuadradino" (1966): Although not directly Brazilian, this piece showcases Ellington's experimentation with Latin-infused rhythms, possibly drawing inspiration from various Latin American musical traditions, including those of Brazil.

8. Quincy Jones: Quincy Jones has incorporated Brazilian musical elements into his productions, infusing his works with the rhythmic vibrancy and melodic richness of Brazilian music, contributing to the cross-pollination of Brazilian and American musical traditions.

Suggested listening

"Soul Bossa Nova" (1962): This iconic instrumental track by Quincy Jones incorporates elements of Bossa Nova, featuring a lively and rhythmic arrangement that reflects his appreciation for Brazilian musical styles.

"Big Band Bossa Nova" (1962): Jones' album "Big Band Bossa Nova" highlights his exploration of Brazilian rhythms within the context of big band arrangements, showcasing his adeptness at blending the energy of big band jazz with the infectious rhythms of Bossa Nova.

"Walking in Space" (1969): While not exclusively Brazilian, this album features elements of Latin and Brazilian musical influences, revealing Jones' experimentation with diverse musical styles and his ability to infuse his compositions with a global sonic palette.

V. Brazilian Jazz 2020s

In recent years, technology has significantly influenced the landscape of Brazilian jazz, fostering new avenues for creative expression and musical innovation. Some of the notable impacts of technology and contemporary trends on Brazilian jazz include:

Digital Innovation and Jazz Production:
The advent of digital recording and production technologies has facilitated the creation of high-quality jazz recordings with enhanced clarity and precision. Brazilian jazz musicians have leveraged digital platforms and software to produce intricately layered compositions, integrating traditional Brazilian elements with modern sonic textures, and enabling a more accessible and streamlined production process.

Contemporary Adaptations and Experimentations:
Contemporary Brazilian jazz artists have embraced technological advancements to experiment with new soundscapes and musical possibilities. This includes the fusion of traditional Brazilian jazz elements with electronic music, creating a dynamic fusion of acoustic and digital sounds. Furthermore, the integration of electronic instruments and digital effects has enabled musicians to push the boundaries of traditional jazz arrangements, fostering a culture of musical experimentation and exploration.

As technology continues to evolve, Brazilian jazz musicians have embraced digital innovation as a means to expand their creative horizons, redefine the boundaries of traditional jazz, and contribute to the ongoing evolution of the genre in the contemporary music landscape.

§

As of the 2020s, the state of jazz in Brazil reflects a dynamic and evolving landscape, characterized by both opportunities and challenges. Some key aspects include:

Challenges

1. Financial Constraints: Jazz musicians in Brazil often face financial challenges due to limited funding opportunities and the economic impact of the global music industry.

2. Limited Audience Reach: Despite a dedicated fan base, expanding the audience for jazz remains a challenge, with mainstream music preferences sometimes overshadowing the genre's growth.

3. Venues and Performance Spaces: Limited access to suitable performance venues can pose challenges for emerging jazz artists, hindering their ability to showcase their talents and reach broader audiences.

Perspectives

1. Diverse Artistic Exploration: Brazilian jazz musicians continue to explore diverse artistic directions, incorporating elements of traditional Brazilian music with modern jazz influences, creating a dynamic and innovative musical fusion.

2. Educational Initiatives: Jazz education programs and workshops have gained prominence, nurturing a new generation of jazz musicians and fostering a deeper understanding of the genre's rich cultural heritage.

3. Collaborative Efforts: Collaborative projects and interdisciplinary initiatives between jazz musicians and artists from other genres have emerged, contributing to the enrichment and diversification of the Brazilian jazz scene.

Changes in Taste

1. Fusion and Experimentation: There has been an increased interest in fusion jazz, blending traditional Brazilian rhythms with contemporary elements, appealing to a diverse range of musical tastes and preferences.

2. Incorporation of Global Trends: Brazilian jazz musicians have incorporated global musical trends into their compositions, infusing their work with a broader international appeal, thereby attracting a more diverse audience.

Venues, Audience, and Festivals

1. Growing Venue Diversity: The emergence of intimate jazz clubs and cultural centers has provided platforms for both established and emerging jazz artists to perform and connect with audiences.

2. Diversifying Audiences: Efforts to diversify audiences through community engagement programs and educational initiatives have helped cultivate a broader appreciation for Brazilian jazz among music enthusiasts and the general public.

3. Festival Culture: Jazz festivals, both local and international, continue to play a significant role in promoting Brazilian jazz culture, providing a platform for artists to showcase their talent and fostering a sense of community within the jazz landscape.

Promotion and Sustainability

1. Digital Platforms and Social Media: Increased use of digital platforms and social media has facilitated the promotion and dissemination of Brazilian jazz, allowing artists to reach global audiences and cultivate a dedicated fan base.

2. Cultural Preservation Efforts: Collaborative efforts between government institutions, cultural organizations, and local communities have been instrumental in preserving and promoting the rich cultural heritage of Brazilian jazz, ensuring its sustainability for future generations.

3. International Collaboration and Exchange: Engaging in international collaborations and exchange programs has helped Brazilian jazz musicians broaden their reach and exposure, contributing to the global promotion and sustainability of Brazilian jazz culture.

§

Looking ahead, Brazilian jazz is poised for an exciting evolution, driven by a new generation of musicians and the emergence of innovative trends within the genre. Some key future directions and emerging trends in Brazilian jazz include:

New Generation of Brazilian Jazz Musicians

1. Diverse Artistic Influences: The upcoming generation of Brazilian jazz musicians is expected to bring a diverse range of artistic influences, incorporating elements from various musical genres and cultural traditions into their compositions and performances.

2. Technological Integration: The integration of modern technological tools and digital platforms is likely to play a pivotal role in the creative process of the new generation of Brazilian jazz musicians, fostering a more dynamic and interactive musical landscape.

Prospects for the Evolution and Expansion of the Genre

1. Innovative Collaborations: Increased collaborations between Brazilian jazz musicians and artists from other genres are expected to redefine the boundaries of the genre, fostering a fusion of diverse musical styles and cultural influences.

2. Global Outreach and Exposure: The global outreach of Brazilian jazz is anticipated to expand, with a growing international audience showing an increased interest in the genre's rich cultural heritage and innovative musical expressions.

3. Cultural Preservation and Education: Ongoing efforts in cultural preservation and jazz education programs are expected to nurture a deeper appreciation for Brazilian jazz among the younger generation, ensuring the continuity of the genre's legacy and artistic contributions.

As Brazilian jazz continues to evolve, the integration of innovative technologies, the cultivation of diverse artistic influences, and the fostering of global collaborations are set to propel the genre into new creative territories, fostering a dynamic and thriving landscape for both musicians and audiences alike.

Chapter 7. Brazilian Orchestral Music

Orchestral influences in Brazilian music are notably influenced by the contributions of classical composers and the incorporation of symphonic interpretations. Some key aspects include:

I. Classical Composers and their Impact

1. Heitor Villa-Lobos: Villa-Lobos, a prominent Brazilian composer, incorporated elements of both Brazilian folk music and Western classical traditions into his compositions, contributing to the development of a distinct Brazilian orchestral style.

2. Antonio Carlos Gomes: Gomes, known for his operatic works, played a significant role in popularizing Brazilian music on the international stage, infusing his compositions with rich orchestral textures and lush harmonies that reflected the cultural richness of Brazil.

Symphonic Interpretations of Brazilian Music

1. Orchestral Arrangements of Popular Songs: Brazilian music has been adapted into symphonic arrangements, incorporating traditional Brazilian rhythms and melodies into the grandeur of orchestral compositions, showcasing the versatility and adaptability of Brazilian musical styles.

2. Fusion of Symphonic and Folk Elements: The fusion of symphonic elements with traditional Brazilian folk music has resulted in the creation of orchestral works that capture the essence of Brazil's diverse musical heritage, transcending boundaries and creating a unique blend of cultural expressions.

Through the contributions of classical composers and the orchestral interpretations of Brazilian music, the integration of symphonic elements has enriched the Brazilian musical landscape, fostering a dynamic interplay between classical traditions and the vibrant rhythms and melodies of Brazil.

Suggested Listening

1. Heitor Villa-Lobos - Bachianas Brasileiras No. 2 (1930)

Listening Note: This composition combines elements of Brazilian folk music with the contrapuntal techniques of Johann Sebastian Bach, creating a rich tapestry of orchestral textures and melodic intricacies.
Recording Dates: Various recordings available; the first recording dates back to the mid-20th century.
Labels: EMI Classics, Deutsche Grammophon, Naxos, among others.

2. Antonio Carlos Gomes - Il Guarany Overture (1870)

Listening Note: Gomes' overture captures the essence of Brazilian folk melodies and rhythms within a grand symphonic framework, reflecting the spirit of Brazilian musical heritage.
Recording Dates: Various recordings available; some dating back to the mid-20th century.
Labels: RCA Victor, Sony Classical, BIS Records, among others.

3. Francisco Mignone - Fantasia Brasileira No. 1 (1929)

Listening Note: Mignone's composition exemplifies a fusion of Brazilian folk influences and European classical traditions, showcasing a vibrant and evocative orchestral work that pays homage to Brazil's cultural richness.
Recording Dates: Various recordings available; recent recordings capture the essence of Mignone's musical legacy.
Labels: BIS Records, Naxos, MEC Records, among others.

4. Camargo Guarnieri - Dança Brasileira (1949)

Listening Note: Guarnieri's "Dança Brasileira" reflects the rhythmic vivacity and dynamic energy of Brazilian dance forms, creating a lively and exuberant orchestral piece that captures the spirit of Brazilian musical celebration.

Recording Dates: Various recordings available, capturing the essence of Guarnieri's musical legacy.
Labels: Naxos, MEC Records, BIS Records, among others.

5. César Guerra-Peixe - Mourão (1952)

Listening Note: Guerra-Peixe's "Mourão" draws inspiration from Brazilian folk music traditions, infusing orchestral textures with the vibrant and rhythmic nuances of Brazilian musical heritage, creating a dynamic and evocative musical narrative.
Recording Dates: Various recordings available; recent recordings capture the essence of Guerra-Peixe's musical legacy.
Labels: BIS Records, Naxos, MEC Records, among others.

Advanced Listening

Here are three additional Brazilian orchestral compositions of note, along with one composition by Egberto Gismonti:

1. Villa-Lobos - Symphony No. 10 "Ameríndia" (1952)

Listening Note: "Ameríndia" exemplifies Villa-Lobos' synthesis of traditional Brazilian and indigenous musical elements within a symphonic framework, creating a compelling narrative that celebrates Brazil's cultural heritage and diversity.
Recording Date: Various recordings available; notable recordings date back to the 20th century.
Label: Sony Classical, Naxos, BIS Records, among others.

2. Ernani Aguiar - Amazonia (1993)

Listening Note: Aguiar's "Amazonia" embodies the lush and exotic landscapes of the Amazon rainforest, fusing orchestral arrangements with Brazilian folk influences, evoking a vibrant and immersive musical journey through the heart of Brazil's natural wonders.
Recording Date: Various recordings available, capturing the essence of Aguiar's musical legacy.
Label: MEC Records, Naxos, BIS Records, among others.

3. Radamés Gnattali - Concerto for Orchestra (1942)

> **Listening Note:** Gnattali's "Concerto for Orchestra" showcases a blend of Brazilian rhythms and classical orchestral techniques, creating a dynamic and expressive musical dialogue that highlights the rich cultural tapestry of Brazil's musical traditions.
> **Recording Dates:** Various recordings available, capturing the essence of Gnattali's musical legacy.
> **Labels:** BIS Records, Naxos, MEC Records, among others.

4. Egberto Gismonti - Academia de Danças (1993)

> **Listening Note:** Gismonti's "Academia de Danças" integrates elements of Brazilian folk music and classical traditions, infusing the orchestral composition with rhythmic vitality and melodic intricacies, reflecting the composer's versatile musical language.
> **Recording Dates:** Various recordings available, capturing Gismonti's innovative approach to orchestral composition.
> **Labels:** ECM Records, Nonesuch Records, EMI Classics, among others.

These compositions collectively represent the diverse and rich tapestry of Brazilian orchestral music, showcasing the depth and creativity of Brazilian composers within the realm of symphonic expression.

II. Actively Listening to Orchestral Music

While listening to Brazilian orchestral works, you can consider the following questions to deepen your understanding and appreciation of the music:

1. Orchestration and Texture: How does the composer utilize different sections of the orchestra to create contrasting textures and layers within the composition?

2. Rhythmic Influences: How do Brazilian rhythmic patterns and dance forms contribute to the overall rhythmic drive and energy of the orchestral work?

3. Melodic Nuances and Phrasing: What melodic motifs or themes are present, and how does the composer develop and transform these melodies throughout the piece?

4. Harmonic Language: What harmonic progressions and tonal colors are employed, and how do they reflect both Brazilian musical traditions and Western classical influences?

5. Cultural and Folk Influences: How does the orchestral work incorporate elements of Brazilian folk music, indigenous music, or regional cultural traditions, and how are these influences expressed within the orchestral framework?

6. Narrative and Emotional Expressiveness: What narrative or emotional journey does the orchestral work evoke, and how does the composer use musical elements to convey a particular mood or atmosphere?

7. Innovation and Tradition: How does the orchestral work balance innovation with traditional compositional techniques, and how does it contribute to the evolution of Brazilian orchestral music within a global context?

8. Sense of Place and Identity: How does the orchestral work capture the essence of Brazil's cultural identity, geography, or natural landscapes, and how does it reflect the country's rich cultural heritage and artistic legacy?

Exploring these questions while listening to Brazilian orchestral works can provide valuable insights into the intricacies of the music, allowing for a deeper appreciation of the compositional techniques and cultural influences embedded within the rich tapestry of Brazilian orchestral music.

§

III. In-Depth Active Listening of **Ernani Aguiar's 'Amazonia'**

Overview

Ernani Aguiar, a prominent Brazilian composer, is celebrated for his contributions to choral music and orchestral compositions. His work often reflects a deep appreciation for Brazil's rich cultural heritage and natural landscapes, with a particular focus on capturing the essence of the Amazon rainforest. One of his notable compositions, "Amazonia," serves as a musical homage to the unparalleled biodiversity and cultural significance of the Amazon region.

"Amazonia" is a symphonic work that intricately weaves together diverse orchestral textures and rhythmic intricacies to evoke the lushness and vitality of the Amazon rainforest. Aguiar's composition embodies the rich tapestry of the Amazon's natural environment, incorporating elements of indigenous musical traditions, vibrant rhythmic patterns, and lush harmonies that pay homage to the region's cultural and ecological diversity.

Through "Amazonia," Aguiar masterfully combines traditional orchestral techniques with indigenous musical influences, creating a captivating musical narrative that captures the vibrant spirit and natural beauty of the Amazon. His innovative orchestration and evocative use of melodies and textures provide listeners with an immersive sonic experience, transporting them into the heart of one of the world's most diverse and awe-inspiring natural landscapes.

Aguiar's dedication to showcasing the cultural significance of the Amazon through music has solidified his position as a leading figure in contemporary Brazilian classical music. "Amazonia" stands as a testament to his artistic vision and his commitment to preserving and celebrating Brazil's rich cultural and ecological heritage through the medium of orchestral composition.

Analysis

i. Orchestration and Texture

"Amazonia" by Ernani Aguiar exhibits a rich orchestration and a textured musical landscape that vividly captures the essence of the Amazon rainforest. Aguiar employs various orchestral techniques to convey the lushness and vibrancy of the Amazon's natural environment.

1. String Section: The strings often create a lush and dense backdrop, symbolizing the thick foliage of the rainforest. Aguiar utilizes rich harmonies and sweeping melodic lines to evoke a sense of the Amazon's expansive and intricate ecosystem.

2. Woodwind and Brass Sections: The woodwind and brass sections frequently interweave intricate melodies and motifs, mimicking the calls of exotic birds and the rustling of leaves in the wind. This adds a dynamic and lively dimension to the orchestral texture, evoking the vibrant life within the rainforest.

3. Percussion: The percussive elements in "Amazonia" are crucial in replicating the rhythmic pulse of the Amazonian environment. Aguiar incorporates a diverse array of percussion instruments, including indigenous drums and shakers, to emulate the rhythmic patterns of tribal music and the natural sounds of the rainforest.

4. Harmonic Colors: Aguiar employs a diverse harmonic palette, utilizing both traditional tonal progressions and more dissonant clusters to convey the contrasts between the serene beauty and the untamed wilderness of the Amazon. This harmonic interplay contributes to the multifaceted texture of the orchestral composition.

Viewed critically and through active listening we find that the orchestration and texture in Ernani Aguiar's "Amazonia" intricately weave together the various elements of the rainforest, creating a vivid sonic representation of the Amazon's biodiversity and cultural richness. The careful orchestral craftsmanship serves to immerse the listener in the enchanting and immersive world of the Brazilian rainforest.

ii. Rhythmic Influences

In Ernani Aguiar's "Amazonia," rhythmic influences play a pivotal role in capturing the essence of the Amazon rainforest. Aguiar skillfully integrates rhythmic patterns and motifs that draw from both indigenous musical traditions and the pulsating energy of the natural environment. These rhythmic influences serve to evoke the dynamic and vibrant spirit of the Amazon region.

1. Indigenous Rhythms: Aguiar incorporates rhythmic elements inspired by indigenous Amazonian music, reflecting the cultural traditions and ceremonial practices of the region's native communities. These rhythmic motifs add an authentic and immersive layer to the composition, paying homage to the rhythmic heritage of the Amazon's indigenous peoples.

2. Natural Soundscape: Aguiar infuses the orchestral arrangement with rhythmic elements that mimic the sounds of the Amazon rainforest, such as the rhythmic patter of rain, the rustling of leaves, and the rhythmic pulse of the region's diverse wildlife. This integration of natural sounds fosters a deep connection between the music and the Amazon's rich ecological tapestry.

3. Percussive Drive: Percussion instruments, including indigenous drums and shakers, contribute to the rhythmic drive of "Amazonia," adding layers of intensity and energy to the composition. Aguiar's use of diverse percussive elements infuses the orchestral arrangement with a pulsating and dynamic rhythmic foundation, mirroring the vitality and liveliness of the Amazon ecosystem.

By drawing on indigenous rhythms, the sounds of nature, and an array of percussive elements, Aguiar adeptly creates a rhythmic tapestry within "Amazonia" that reflects the cultural vibrancy and natural vitality of the Amazon rainforest. The intricate rhythmic influences serve to immerse listeners in the captivating and immersive world of the Amazon's diverse and pulsating musical landscape.

iii. Melodic Nuances and Phrasing

In "Amazonia," melodic nuances and phrasing are carefully crafted to reflect the richness and diversity of the Amazon rainforest.

Aguiar's composition weaves intricate melodies and expressive phrasing that capture the essence of the region's natural beauty and cultural heritage. Through his use of evocative melodic motifs and nuanced phrasing, Aguiar creates a compelling musical narrative that resonates with the vibrant spirit of the Amazon.

1. Evocative Melodic Motifs: Aguiar employs evocative melodic motifs that echo the enchanting sounds of the Amazon, drawing inspiration from indigenous musical traditions and the diverse wildlife of the rainforest. These motifs serve to evoke a sense of wonder and exploration, transporting listeners to the heart of the Amazon's lush and vibrant landscapes.

2. Expressive Phrasing: Aguiar's expressive phrasing captures the ebb and flow of the Amazon's natural rhythms, mirroring the undulating movements of the rainforest and the interplay of light and shadow within its dense foliage. Through nuanced phrasing, he conveys a sense of dynamism and fluidity, reflecting the ever-changing and organic nature of the Amazonian ecosystem.

3. Cultural Allusions: Aguiar integrates melodic nuances that allude to the cultural heritage and folklore of the Amazon, infusing the composition with echoes of indigenous songs and traditional melodies. These melodic references serve as a testament to the rich cultural tapestry of the region, celebrating the diversity and resilience of the Amazon's cultural legacy.

Through the use of evocative melodic motifs, expressive phrasing, and cultural allusions, Aguiar's "Amazonia" encapsulates the intricate melodic tapestry of the Amazon rainforest, capturing its allure and mystique through a harmonious interplay of musical expressions. The melodic nuances and phrasing in the composition serve as a testament to Aguiar's profound musical craftsmanship and his ability to evoke the essence of the Amazon's natural and cultural wonders through the language of music.

iv. Harmonic Language

In Ernani Aguiar's "Amazonia," the harmonic language is thoughtfully crafted to mirror the lush and diverse landscapes of the Amazon rainforest. Aguiar's harmonic choices evoke the natural splendor of the region while paying homage to the cultural and indigenous traditions that thrive within its boundaries. Through a carefully curated harmonic palette, Aguiar creates a musical narrative that reflects the depth and richness of the Amazon's ecological and cultural tapestry.

1. Blend of Traditional and Exotic Harmonies: Aguiar blends traditional Western classical harmonies with exotic, modal, and pentatonic scales that reflect the tonal colors and folk music traditions of the Amazon region. This fusion of harmonies creates a vibrant and eclectic sonic landscape, symbolizing the interplay between the contemporary and the ancient within the rainforest.

2. Colorful and Textured Progressions: Aguiar's use of colorful and textured harmonic progressions mirrors the rich biodiversity and complexity of the Amazon ecosystem. He employs lush and intricate chord voicings that evoke the vibrant flora and fauna of the rainforest, creating a harmonic backdrop that is both immersive and dynamic.

3. Expressive Dissonances and Resolutions: Aguiar artfully integrates moments of expressive dissonance and resolution to evoke the contrasting experiences of tranquility and unpredictability found in the Amazon. The interplay between dissonant and consonant harmonies reflects the dichotomy between the serene beauty and the untamed wilderness of the rainforest, creating a harmonic language that embodies the duality of the Amazon's natural environment.

By blending traditional and exotic harmonies, creating colorful and textured progressions, and incorporating expressive dissonances and resolutions, Aguiar's harmonic language in "Amazonia" paints a vivid musical portrait of the Amazon rainforest, capturing its breathtaking beauty, cultural richness, and ecological complexity within the framework of a symphonic composition.

v. Cultural and Folk Influences

In "Amazonia," cultural and folk influences are interwoven into the fabric of the composition, reflecting the rich tapestry of indigenous traditions and cultural heritage found within the Amazon rainforest. Aguiar's incorporation of cultural and folk elements serves to celebrate the diversity of Amazonian culture and pay homage to the region's vibrant and dynamic communities.

1. Indigenous Musical Traditions: Aguiar draws inspiration from the musical traditions of indigenous Amazonian communities, incorporating rhythmic patterns, melodic motifs, and ceremonial elements that echo the cultural practices and musical expressions of the region's native inhabitants. These influences imbue the composition with an authentic and immersive portrayal of Amazonian cultural heritage.

2. Folkloric Rhythms and Instruments: Aguiar integrates folkloric rhythms and indigenous instruments into the orchestral arrangement, evoking the spirit of Amazonian folklore and the pulsating energy of traditional music and dance rituals. By infusing the composition with the sounds of native percussion and wind instruments, he honors the cultural significance of these musical traditions within the Amazonian community.

3. Regional Musical Narratives: Aguiar weaves regional musical narratives into "Amazonia," highlighting the interconnectedness of the Amazon rainforest with the cultural identities and oral histories of its diverse communities. His incorporation of thematic elements and musical storytelling captures the essence of Amazonian cultural narratives, emphasizing the symbiotic relationship between the natural world and human experiences within the rainforest.

Through the integration of indigenous musical traditions, folkloric rhythms and instruments, and regional musical narratives, Aguiar's "Amazonia" serves as a testament to the rich cultural heritage and artistic legacy of the Amazon rainforest. His thoughtful incorporation of cultural and folk influences underscores the importance of preserving and celebrating the vibrant cultural tapestry that thrives within the heart of the Amazon.

vi. Narrative And Emotive Expressiveness

In Ernani Aguiar's "Amazonia," narrative and emotional expressiveness play a vital role in conveying the rich tapestry of the Amazon rainforest's natural beauty and cultural significance. Aguiar's orchestral composition weaves a compelling narrative that evokes a range of emotions, inviting listeners to embark on an immersive musical journey through the diverse landscapes and vibrant communities of the Amazon.

1. Evocative Nature Imagery: Aguiar's use of evocative musical motifs and dynamic orchestrations paints a vivid sonic portrait of the Amazon's lush foliage, winding rivers, and diverse wildlife. The composition's narrative structure reflects the ebb and flow of life within the rainforest, imbuing the music with a sense of organic growth and movement.

2. Journey of Discovery: Aguiar's orchestral arrangement takes listeners on a journey of discovery, inviting them to explore the depths of the Amazon's cultural heritage and ecological wonders. Through shifts in tempo, dynamics, and melodic development, the composition guides the listener through a narrative arc that mirrors the awe-inspiring and transformative experiences of encountering the rainforest's natural splendor.

3. Cultural Resonance and Unity: The emotional expressiveness of "Amazonia" resonates with themes of cultural resilience and unity, highlighting the interconnectedness between human communities and the natural world. Aguiar's use of poignant melodic phrasing and harmonies underscores the symbiotic relationship between cultural traditions, ecological preservation, and emotional resonance within the Amazonian context.

vii. Balancing Innovation with Traditional Compositional Techniques

By infusing the orchestral composition with evocative nature imagery, a journey of discovery, and themes of cultural resonance and unity, Aguiar masterfully conveys a narrative that transcends the boundaries of musical expression, inviting listeners to engage with the emotional depth and poignant storytelling embedded within the vibrant soundscape of the Amazon rainforest. In "Amazonia," Ernani Aguiar expertly balances innovation with traditional compositional techniques, creating a harmonious synthesis of contemporary orchestral expression and the rich musical heritage of the Amazon region. Aguiar's orchestral work demonstrates a meticulous interplay between innovative musical approaches and classical foundations, striking a delicate balance that amplifies the composition's cultural resonance and artistic depth.

1. Innovative Orchestration and Instrumentation: Aguiar integrates innovative orchestration and instrumentation techniques that expand the sonic palette of the composition, infusing it with contemporary tonal colors and textures while remaining rooted in the orchestral tradition. His use of unconventional timbres and instrumental combinations contributes to the modern sensibility of the work, adding a layer of creative ingenuity to the overall orchestral landscape.

2. Traditional Rhythmic and Melodic Motifs: While exploring innovative avenues, Aguiar incorporates traditional rhythmic and melodic motifs derived from Amazonian folk music and indigenous cultural practices. These motifs serve as the foundation for the composition, grounding the work in the authentic musical traditions of the region and fostering a deep connection to the Amazon's cultural heritage.

3. Dynamic Harmonic Progressions and Structures: Aguiar employs dynamic harmonic progressions and structures that integrate both traditional tonal systems and contemporary harmonic explorations. By seamlessly blending traditional harmonic idioms with innovative harmonic techniques, he creates a musical language that resonates with both classical and modern audiences, fostering an inclusive and accessible listening experience.

Through a thoughtful amalgamation of innovative orchestration, traditional rhythmic and melodic motifs, and dynamic harmonic progressions, Aguiar's "Amazonia" exemplifies a seamless integration of innovation and tradition, showcasing his ability to bridge the gap between classical composition and contemporary musical expression. The balanced interplay of these elements contributes to the composition's distinctive and multifaceted musical identity, highlighting the enduring relevance of the Amazon's cultural legacy within a contemporary artistic context.

viii. Sense of Place and Identity

In "Amazonia," the orchestral work serves as a poignant reflection of Brazil's cultural identity, geography, and natural landscapes, encapsulating the rich tapestry of the country's diverse heritage and artistic legacy. Aguiar's composition resonates with the essence of Brazil's cultural narrative, evoking a profound sense of place and belonging within the Amazon rainforest's vibrant and ecologically diverse ecosystem.

1. Celebration of Cultural Diversity: "Amazonia" celebrates Brazil's cultural diversity by incorporating elements of indigenous musical traditions, folklore, and regional customs. Through its thematic exploration of cultural expressions and rituals, the orchestral work pays tribute to the multiplicity of cultural identities that contribute to the vibrant mosaic of Brazilian society.

2. Evoke Geographic Splendor: Aguiar's orchestral arrangement evokes the geographic splendor of Brazil's natural landscapes, capturing the breathtaking beauty of the Amazon's lush rainforests, winding rivers, and exotic wildlife. The composition's immersive sonic imagery serves as a testament to the country's diverse topography and its status as a global hub of biodiversity and ecological richness.

3. Legacy of Artistic Expression: By weaving together indigenous musical motifs, classical orchestrations, and contemporary compositional techniques, "Amazonia" reflects Brazil's rich legacy of artistic expression and creative innovation. Aguiar's orchestral work not only pays homage to the country's artistic heritage but also reinforces the continued evolution of Brazil's cultural legacy within the realm of symphonic composition.

Through its celebration of cultural diversity, evocation of geographic splendor, and reflection of Brazil's artistic legacy, Aguiar's "Amazonia" stands as a testament to the enduring significance of Brazil's cultural identity and natural landscapes. The orchestral work serves as a timeless homage to the country's rich heritage and underscores the vital role of artistic expression in preserving and promoting Brazil's cultural legacy on the global stage.

IV. Why do we Analyze and Actively Listen to Orchestral Music?

We analyze music and actively listen to orchestral works, seeking nuance and subtle distinctions, to unlock the profound emotional and intellectual depths embedded within the fabric of musical compositions. Through analytical engagement, we delve into the intricacies of a piece, unraveling its layers of meaning and uncovering the intricate techniques employed by the composer to evoke specific moods, narratives, and cultural references.

1. Cognitive Engagement and Interpretation: Analyzing music encourages cognitive engagement, allowing us to interpret and decipher the underlying musical structures, harmonic progressions, and rhythmic complexities that contribute to the overall sonic experience. By actively listening and seeking nuances, we gain a deeper understanding of the composer's artistic intent and the emotional resonance of the orchestral work.

2. Appreciation of Artistic Craftsmanship: Delving into the nuances of an orchestral composition enables us to appreciate the artistic craftsmanship and technical mastery involved in its creation. By discerning the subtle variations in instrumentation, dynamics, and phrasing, we recognize the meticulous attention to detail and the creative ingenuity that contribute to the composition's aesthetic appeal and artistic merit.

3. Cultural and Historical Context: Analyzing orchestral works allows us to situate the music within its cultural and historical context, unveiling the socio-cultural influences, musical traditions, and thematic narratives that inform the composition's overarching message. Through nuanced listening, we gain insight into the cultural nuances and historical references embedded within the music, fostering a deeper appreciation for the societal and artistic underpinnings of the orchestral work.

4. Personal and Emotional Connection: Actively listening to orchestral works and seeking subtleties enables us to forge a personal and emotional connection with the music, allowing us to resonate with its expressive power and transformative potential. By immersing ourselves in the nuances of the composition, we become attuned to its evocative qualities and its capacity to evoke a range of emotional responses, fostering a profound and intimate relationship between the listener and the music.

In essence, the analysis of music and the active listening of orchestral works, with a focus on uncovering nuance and subtle distinctions, allows us to explore the depths of artistic expression, cultural significance, and emotional resonance embedded within the intricate tapestry of sound. Through this process, we not only enrich our understanding of the music but also deepen our connection to the profound and transcendent language of orchestral composition.

V. The Future of Orchestral Music in Brazil

The future of orchestral music in Brazil presents both challenges and promising prospects, with a growing emphasis on nurturing emerging talent and expanding the reach of orchestral ensembles across the country. While facing various obstacles, the Brazilian orchestral scene continues to exhibit resilience and a commitment to innovation, fostering a dynamic environment for the cultivation of new artistic voices and the preservation of cultural heritage.

Challenges:

1. Funding and Infrastructure: Limited financial resources and infrastructure constraints pose significant challenges to the sustainability and expansion of orchestral music in Brazil. Ensuring adequate funding for orchestras, concert venues, and educational programs remains a critical concern for the long-term development of the orchestral landscape.

2. Access and Outreach: Enhancing access to orchestral performances in remote and underserved communities is a persistent challenge, as geographical barriers and socioeconomic disparities often hinder widespread audience engagement. Efforts to promote inclusivity and expand outreach initiatives are essential for fostering a more diverse and accessible orchestral culture.

3. Educational Support: Strengthening music education programs and fostering collaboration between educational institutions and orchestras are crucial for nurturing the next generation of Brazilian musicians. Investing in comprehensive music education, mentorship programs, and specialized training opportunities can help cultivate a vibrant and skilled pool of emerging talent.

Upcoming Talent and Promising Initiatives:

1. Youth Orchestras and Education Programs: The rise of youth orchestras and educational initiatives across Brazil demonstrates a growing commitment to cultivating young talent and fostering a deep appreciation for orchestral music. These programs play a pivotal role in providing aspiring musicians with the necessary resources, mentorship, and performance opportunities to hone their skills and contribute to the future of Brazilian orchestral music.

2. Collaborative Partnerships and Cultural Exchanges: Collaborative partnerships between Brazilian orchestras, international ensembles, and renowned conductors and composers foster a spirit of artistic exchange and promote the global visibility of Brazilian orchestral talent. These collaborations not only showcase the diversity and richness of Brazil's musical heritage but also provide emerging musicians with invaluable opportunities for artistic growth and international recognition.

3. Technological Integration and Digital Platforms: Leveraging technological advancements and digital platforms to enhance audience engagement, promote cultural accessibility, and facilitate virtual performances and educational resources can expand the reach and impact of Brazilian orchestral music. Embracing digital innovation enables orchestras to connect with diverse audiences and adapt to evolving trends in the global music landscape.

By addressing key challenges and harnessing the potential of upcoming talent and innovative initiatives, the future of orchestral music in Brazil holds the promise of artistic vibrancy, cultural enrichment, and a continued legacy of musical excellence that resonates both nationally and internationally.

VI. Additional Significant Orchestral Music in Brazil

1. Claudio Santoro - Symphony No. 4 (1953)
- Claudio Santoro was a Brazilian composer and conductor recognized for his contributions to contemporary classical music. His Symphony No. 4 showcases his mastery of orchestration and complex musical structures.

2. Camargo Guarnieri - Abertura Concertante (1945)
- Camargo Guarnieri was an influential Brazilian composer known for his distinct nationalistic style. "Abertura Concertante" exemplifies his unique blend of traditional Brazilian themes with modern compositional techniques.

3. Francisco Mignone - Maracatu de Chico Rei (1945)
- Francisco Mignone was a renowned Brazilian composer and conductor celebrated for his innovative approach to incorporating Brazilian folk elements into symphonic compositions. "Maracatu de Chico Rei" is a vibrant representation of his distinctive style.

4. Alberto Nepomuceno - Série Brasileira (1898)
- Alberto Nepomuceno was a significant figure in Brazilian music history, recognized for his efforts to promote a national identity in classical music. "Série Brasileira" reflects his incorporation of Brazilian folk themes into orchestral arrangements.

5. Egberto Gismonti - Dança das Cabeças (1977)
- Egberto Gismonti is a renowned Brazilian composer and multi-instrumentalist known for his diverse musical influences. "Dança das Cabeças" represents his experimental and innovative approach to symphonic composition.

6. Oscar Lorenzo Fernandez - Batuque (1926)
- Oscar Lorenzo Fernandez was a Brazilian composer and conductor known for his contributions to Brazilian art music. "Batuque" is a significant work that showcases Fernandez's integration of Afro-Brazilian rhythms into classical symphonic music.

7. Ernani Aguiar - Tocata (1981)

- Ernani Aguiar is a Brazilian composer recognized for his eclectic musical style. "Tocata" demonstrates his ability to combine traditional Brazilian elements with contemporary symphonic techniques.

8. Edino Krieger - Maracatu de Manaus (1957)

- Edino Krieger was a Brazilian composer known for his diverse body of work, encompassing various musical genres. "Maracatu de Manaus" is a notable piece that highlights Krieger's fusion of Brazilian folk music with symphonic elements.

9. Alberto Ginastera - Panambi (1937)

- Although born in Argentina, Alberto Ginastera had a significant influence on Brazilian music. "Panambi" is an important orchestral work by Ginastera that showcases his exploration of indigenous South American themes and rhythms.

10. Carlos Gomes - Symphony in F Major (1869)

- Antonio Carlos Gomes was a renowned 19th-century Brazilian opera composer. His Symphony in F Major reflects his early contributions to Brazilian classical music and exhibits elements of both European and Brazilian musical styles.

11. Almeida Prado - Cartas Celestes (1978)

- Almeida Prado was a Brazilian composer celebrated for his modernist approach to classical music. "Cartas Celestes" is a significant symphonic work that reflects Prado's exploration of unconventional harmonies and orchestral textures.

12. Marlos Nobre - Concerto for Orchestra (1971)

- Marlos Nobre is a prominent Brazilian composer known for his contemporary and experimental compositions. His "Concerto for Orchestra" is a testament to his innovative orchestral techniques and complex musical structures.

13. Gilberto Mendes - Suite Vila Rica (1959)

- Gilberto Mendes was a Brazilian composer recognized for his avant-garde and experimental musical style. "Suite Vila Rica" is a significant symphonic work that reflects Mendes's exploration of unconventional tonalities and rhythmic complexities.

14. Henrique Oswald - Rustic Concert Piece (1898)
- Henrique Oswald was a Brazilian composer of Swiss descent known for his contributions to Brazilian classical music. "Rustic Concert Piece" is one of his notable works, exemplifying his mastery of orchestration and classical form.

15. Joao Guilherme Ripper - Cenas Infantis (1994)
- Joao Guilherme Ripper is a contemporary Brazilian composer known for his diverse and expressive musical language. "Cenas Infantis" is a notable symphonic work that reflects Ripper's exploration of childhood themes through orchestral music.

16. Marisa Rezende - A Menina das Nuvens (1984)
- Marisa Rezende is a prominent Brazilian composer recognized for her contributions to contemporary classical music. "A Menina das Nuvens" is a significant symphonic work that showcases Rezende's evocative and expressive musical style.

17. Osvaldo Lacerda - Symphony No. 2 (1961)
- Osvaldo Lacerda was a celebrated Brazilian composer known for his contributions to Brazilian classical music education. His Symphony No. 2 is a significant work that demonstrates Lacerda's mastery of symphonic form and orchestration.

18. Mozart Camargo Guarnieri - Symphony No. 4 (1953)
- Mozart Camargo Guarnieri was an influential Brazilian composer celebrated for his nationalistic approach to classical music. His Symphony No. 4 reflects his mastery of symphonic structure and his incorporation of Brazilian folk elements into orchestral compositions.

19. "Uirapuru: Symphony of the Amazon" by Heitor Villa-Lobos (1935)
- Villa-Lobos, a prominent figure in Brazilian classical music, composed "Uirapuru: Symphony of the Amazon" as an homage to the rich biodiversity and cultural heritage of the Amazon rainforest. This symphony intricately weaves together lush orchestral textures, indigenous melodies, and folkloric influences, evoking the enchanting soundscape of the Amazon's vibrant ecosystem. Through its dynamic movements and evocative sonic imagery, "Uirapuru" captures the essence of the Amazon's mystical allure and serves as a testament to Villa-Lobos's enduring legacy in Brazilian orchestral composition.

20. "Memórias do Brasil" by Camargo Guarnieri (1965)

- "Memórias do Brasil" is a captivating orchestral suite by Camargo Guarnieri that embodies a nostalgic reflection on Brazil's cultural history and musical traditions. Inspired by the rich tapestry of Brazilian folklore and regional customs, Guarnieri's composition interweaves thematic elements and melodic motifs drawn from diverse Brazilian musical genres, creating a sonic portrait that celebrates the country's cultural resilience and artistic heritage. Through its evocative melodies and expressive orchestrations, "Memórias do Brasil" encapsulates the essence of Brazil's multifaceted cultural identity and pays tribute to the enduring spirit of its people.

These orchestral compositions, though relatively obscure, represent the profound artistic contributions of Villa-Lobos and Guarnieri to the rich tapestry of Brazilian orchestral music, showcasing their mastery in crafting symphonic narratives that resonate with the cultural and natural landscapes of Brazil.

Final Thoughts

As we conclude our exploration of Brazilian music from a humanities perspective, it is evident that the influence of this rich and vibrant musical tradition extends far beyond the boundaries of its homeland. Throughout our journey, we have witnessed the dynamic interplay of cultural narratives, historical legacies, and artistic expressions that have shaped Brazil's musical landscape and propelled its influence onto the global stage. From the pulsating rhythms of Samba and Bossa Nova to the intricate harmonies of MPB and the evocative melodies of Brazilian Jazz, the multifaceted tapestry of Brazilian music continues to resonate with audiences worldwide, transcending linguistic and cultural barriers to foster a universal language of creativity and human connection.

The profound legacy of Brazilian music on the world stage is exemplified through the spirit of collaboration and cultural exchange that has permeated international music scenes. Brazilian artists have forged meaningful partnerships with musicians from diverse backgrounds, fostering a global dialogue that celebrates the shared ethos of artistic exploration and mutual inspiration. From the iconic collaborations of Brazilian and international jazz virtuosos to the fusion of Brazilian rhythms with the sounds of contemporary pop and rock, these musical encounters have not only enriched the global sonic landscape but have also underscored the enduring appeal of Brazilian music as a catalyst for cross-cultural understanding and creative innovation.

Moreover, the impact of Brazilian music on world music at large resonates with its ability to transcend geographical borders and cultural divides, serving as a powerful conduit for the dissemination of Brazilian cultural heritage and the promotion of cultural diversity. The rhythmic vibrancy, melodic intricacies, and lyrical poignancy embedded within the fabric of Brazilian music have left an indelible mark on the broader tapestry of world music, inspiring artists and audiences alike to embrace the universal values of harmony, diversity, and artistic expression.

As we reflect on the enduring legacy of Brazilian music and its profound impact on the global stage, let us embrace the spirit of cultural exchange and artistic dialogue that continues to define the essence of Brazilian musical heritage. Through our collective appreciation for the transcendent power of music, may we honor the legacy of Brazilian musicians and their invaluable contributions to the world of music, fostering a global community that celebrates the richness of cultural expression and the transformative potential of artistic unity.

Author's Personal Favourites

Egberto Gismonti

Introduction to Egberto Gismonti:
Egberto Gismonti was born on December 5, 1947, in Carmo, Brazil. His musical journey has been marked by a profound exploration of Brazil's diverse cultural and musical traditions. From a young age, he exhibited exceptional talent as a pianist and guitarist, later mastering an array of instruments such as the guitar, flute, and more.

Musical Influences:
Gismonti's music is a reflection of Brazil's rich and multifaceted musical landscape. He draws inspiration from the traditional sounds of Brazil, incorporating elements of choro, samba, and bossa nova, while also embracing global influences. His compositions often evoke the beauty of the Amazon rainforest, the rhythms of Afro-Brazilian traditions, and the intricacies of European classical music.

Notable Contributions:
1. **"Dança das Cabeças" (Dance of the Heads):** A collaboration with percussionist Nana Vasconcelos, this album fuses African rhythms with Brazilian melodies, creating a mesmerizing and percussion-driven soundscape.

2. **"Carmen" (with the Norwegian Chamber Orchestra):**
Gismonti's collaboration with the Norwegian Chamber Orchestra showcases his ability to seamlessly blend classical and Brazilian music, offering a fresh perspective on both traditions.

3. **"Solo" (1979):** In this solo guitar album, Gismonti showcases his virtuosity and composition skills, weaving intricate and emotive melodies.

4. **"Meeting Point" (1984):** An exploration of world music, this album brings together musicians from various cultures, highlighting Gismonti's commitment to global musical dialogues.

Playlist for Egberto Gismonti:

To truly appreciate the breadth of Gismonti's work, I've curated a short playlist of some of his most influential and evocative compositions:

1. "Loro" (1981, ECM Records) - A gentle and introspective piece that beautifully showcases Gismonti's guitar virtuosity.

2. "Frevo" (1977, EMI-Odeon)- An exhilarating foray into the rhythms of Brazilian carnival music, featuring his signature fusion of jazz and Brazilian folk elements.

3. "Água e Vinho" (1972, EMI-Odeon) - A delicate and contemplative piece that highlights Gismonti's sensitivity as a pianist and composer.

4. "Baião Malandro" (on the album "Cigano" in 1984, EMI-Odeon) - An exploration of the baião rhythm, blending traditional Brazilian elements with modern jazz improvisation.

5. "Raga"(on "Dança Das Cabeças" in 1977, ECM Records) - An example of Gismonti's experimentation with Indian classical music, demonstrating his willingness to cross cultural boundaries.

These selections offer a glimpse into the remarkable musical journey of Egberto Gismonti, a musician whose work transcends genres and borders, inviting us to explore the rich tapestry of Brazilian music and beyond. Enjoy the journey through his captivating soundscape.

Duas Vozes. Egberto Gismonti and Nana Vasconcelos. 1985. ECM Records, CD.

"Duas Vozes" is a collaborative album by Brazilian musicians Egberto Gismonti and Nana Vasconcelos, released in 1985. The album features a blend of jazz, Latin jazz, and fusion, with elements of Brazilian folk music. Here are some listening notes and an overview of the album:

Tracklist:
1. Aquarela Do Brasil
2. Rio De Janeiro
3. Tomarapeba
4. Dançando
5. Fogueira
6. Bianca
7. Don Quixote
8. O Dia, À Noite

Overview:
"Duas Vozes" is a beautiful and timeless album that showcases the musical chemistry between Gismonti and Vasconcelos. The album features Gismonti on guitar, piano, dilruba, flute, and voice, while Vasconcelos plays percussion, berimbau, and voice. The album's sound is characterized by its use of Brazilian folk music elements, such as the use of traditional Amazonian songs in "Tomarapeba." The album also features a cover of "Aquarela Do Brasil," a classic Brazilian song composed by Ary Barroso. The album's sound is gentle, low-key, and psychedelic, with plenty of subtle flourishes and folk lyricism.

Listening notes:
- "Aquarela Do Brasil" is a beautiful and upbeat rendition of the classic Brazilian song. The song features Gismonti's intricate guitar work and Vasconcelos' percussive rhythms.

- "Rio De Janeiro" is a slow and contemplative piece that features Gismonti's piano and Vasconcelos' berimbau.

- "Tomarapeba" is a haunting and atmospheric piece that features traditional Amazonian songs and Vasconcelos' percussion.

- "Dançando" is an upbeat and rhythmic piece that features Gismonti's guitar and Vasconcelos' percussion.

- "Fogueira" is a slow and melancholic piece that features Gismonti's guitar and Vasconcelos' voice.

- "Bianca" is a beautiful and ethereal piece that features Gismonti's flute and Vasconcelos' percussion.

- "Don Quixote" is a complex and dynamic piece that features Gismonti's guitar and Carneiro's percussion.

- "O Dia, À Noite" is a slow and atmospheric piece that features Vasconcelos' voice and percussion.

"Duas Vozes" is a beautiful and captivating album that showcases the musical talents of Gismonti and Vasconcelos. The album's blend of jazz, Latin jazz, and Brazilian folk music elements creates a unique and timeless sound that is both relaxing and engaging.

Naná Vasconcelos

Introduction to Naná Vasconcelos:
Naná Vasconcelos, born on August 2, 1944, in Recife, Brazil, was a master of percussion and a musical explorer. His journey began with traditional Brazilian rhythms and extended to embrace a multitude of global influences, from African and Middle Eastern percussion to jazz and contemporary music.

The Art of Percussion:
Vasconcelos was a virtuoso of the berimbau, a Brazilian musical bow, and a master of various percussion instruments, including the djembe, congas, and talking drum. He was renowned for his ability to coax intricate melodies and harmonies from percussion instruments, blurring the lines between rhythm and melody.

Notable Contributions:
1. "Berimbau Solo" (1976): A groundbreaking album where Vasconcelos explores the sonic possibilities of the berimbau, demonstrating his mastery of this iconic Brazilian instrument.

2. "Saudades" (1980, ECM): In this album, Vasconcelos collaborates with Brazilian musicians and jazz artists, creating a fusion of rhythms that transcends borders.

3. "Bush Dance" (1986, Antilles Records): A collaboration with Australian musicians, this album combines Aboriginal rhythms with Vasconcelos' percussion wizardry, resulting in a mesmerizing musical dialogue.

4. "Storytelling" (1992, Hemisphere): An exploration of African rhythms, this album features Vasconcelos' mesmerizing djembe and percussion work, bridging continents and cultures.

Playlist for Naná Vasconcelos:

To immerse ourselves in the rhythmic artistry of Naná Vasconcelos, I've put together a short playlist of some of his most compelling and innovative compositions:

1. **"Amazon River"** - A hypnotic and atmospheric piece featuring Vasconcelos' berimbau and percussion, evoking the spirit of the Amazon rainforest. The song has been featured on various albums, including "Amazonas" (1973) and "Amazon" (1980).

2. **"Mingus in the Jungles of Brazil"** - A collaboration with Charles Mingus that showcases Vasconcelos' ability to blend jazz and Brazilian rhythms seamlessly. This song is part of "Suadades"

3. **"Rain Dance" (1989, Antilles New Directions)** - An electrifying djembe performance that demonstrates Vasconcelos' mastery of African percussion.

4. **"Trilhas" (2006, Azul Music)** - A composition that melds Brazilian and Middle Eastern influences, highlighting Vasconcelos' versatility.

5. **"As Falls Wichita, So Falls Wichita Falls" (1981, ECM)** - Naná Vasconcelos, makes a significant contribution to the iconic album "As Falls Wichita, So Falls Wichita Falls", a collaboration between the celebrated American jazz artist Pat Metheny and the multifaceted composer Lyle Mays, released in 1981.

Vasconcelos's percussion work on the album added a rich layer of Brazilian and Afro-Brazilian rhythms, infusing the compositions with a vibrant and eclectic energy. His masterful utilization of various percussion instruments, including the berimbau, congas, and various traditional Brazilian percussion elements, created a dynamic and immersive sonic landscape that complemented Metheny's intricate guitar work and Mays's nuanced compositions.

Through his collaborative efforts on "As Falls Wichita, So Falls Wichita Falls," Vasconcelos not only contributed to the album's diverse cultural influences but also showcased his unparalleled ability to seamlessly blend traditional Brazilian rhythms with contemporary jazz sensibilities. His unique musical voice added a distinct and enriching dimension to the album, solidifying the record as a timeless and groundbreaking fusion of diverse musical traditions.

These selections offer a glimpse into the mesmerizing and innovative world of Naná Vasconcelos, a percussionist and composer who broke boundaries and continues to inspire musicians and percussionists worldwide. Enjoy the rhythmic journey through his extraordinary music.

Codona

Codona was a collaborative group that emerged in the late 1970s, comprising three prominent musicians: Colin Walcott, Don Cherry, and Nana Vasconcelos. The trio, known for their diverse cultural backgrounds and musical influences, created a unique fusion of world music, jazz, and avant-garde styles.

Their self-titled album, "Codona," released in 1979, by ECM showcased their shared passion for cross-cultural musical exploration, incorporating elements of traditional Indian, African, and Brazilian music. Codona's music was characterized by its rich textures, intricate rhythms, and improvisational spirit, creating a captivating and transcendent sonic experience for listeners.

While their collaboration was relatively short-lived, Codona's innovative approach to fusion music left a lasting legacy, influencing subsequent generations of musicians and contributing to the broader development of world music as a genre. The group's self-titled album, "Codona," remains a celebrated and influential work, reflecting the trio's collective artistry and their shared commitment to pushing the boundaries of conventional musical expression.

Airto Moreira

Airto Moreira, commonly known as Airto, is a Brazilian percussionist and drummer known for his contributions to jazz, world music, and fusion. He was born on August 5, 1941, in Itaiópolis, Brazil. Airto is renowned for his innovative and versatile percussion work, which has enriched numerous musical genres. Here's a brief bio and a selected discography highlighting some of his notable works:

Bio:
- Airto began his musical journey in Brazil, where he was exposed to traditional Brazilian rhythms and percussion instruments from a young age.
- In the 1960s, he moved to the United States and quickly established himself as a sought-after percussionist in the jazz and fusion scenes.
- He gained prominence through his collaborations with artists like Miles Davis, Weather Report, and Chick Corea's Return to Forever.
- Airto's playing style is characterized by its rhythmic complexity, use of Brazilian percussion instruments, and his ability to blend various cultural influences into his music.

Selected Discography:

1. "Fingers" (1973, CTI Records): Airto's debut album as a bandleader is a fusion of jazz, Latin, and Brazilian rhythms. It features Chick Corea, Stanley Clarke, and other notable musicians.

2. "Return to Forever" - Return to Forever (1972, ECM): Airto joined Chick Corea's Return to Forever, contributing his percussive talents to this landmark fusion album.

3. "Virgin Land" (1974, Warner Bros. Records) - is a studio album by the Brazilian percussionist Airto Moreira, released in 1974. The album, known for its fusion of jazz, Brazilian, and Latin musical elements, underscores Airto's prowess as a versatile musician and his ability to seamlessly integrate diverse cultural influences into his compositions.

At the time of its release, "Virgin Land" was under the prestigious Warner Bros. Records label, contributing to its widespread recognition within the global music community. The album not only solidified Airto's reputation as a trailblazing percussionist but also served as a testament to his innovative approach to music-making, highlighting his unique ability to bridge cultural divides and create a captivating fusion of sounds that resonated with audiences across various musical genres.

4. "The Hissing of Summer Lawns" (1975, Asylum Records):
Airto's rhythmic expertise and intricate percussion work added a distinctive Brazilian flair to the album, enriching the sonic landscape of Mitchell's groundbreaking folk and jazz-infused compositions.

Airto's collaboration with Joni Mitchell further highlighted his ability to infuse diverse musical styles and cultural influences into the fabric of contemporary music. His dynamic contributions on the album served as a testament to his versatility and profound understanding of rhythmic intricacies, elevating the overall musical experience and contributing to the album's enduring legacy in the realm of folk and jazz fusion.

5. "I'm Fine, How Are You?" (1977, Warner Bros. Records):
Another collaboration with Flora Purim, this album blends jazz, Latin, and Brazilian styles.

6. "Touching You... Touching Me" (1979, Warner Bros. Records):
Airto explored a more eclectic sound on this album, incorporating elements of funk, jazz, and world music.

7. "Three-Way Mirror" (1985, Reference Recordings): In this
album, Airto collaborated with percussionists Flora Purim and Joe Farrell, offering a fusion of their respective styles.

One lesser-known track by Airto Moreira is "Lydia at 90," a captivating composition that exemplifies Airto's intricate percussion work and his ability to infuse diverse cultural influences into his music. Released in 1983 on the album "Three-Way Mirror," this deep cut showcases Airto's dynamic rhythmic sensibilities and his innovative approach to blending Brazilian rhythms with contemporary jazz elements. "Lydia at 90" stands as a testament to Airto's musical versatility and his enduring legacy as a pioneering figure in the realm of world music and percussion.

8. "Aluê" (2016, ECM): "Aluê" is a notable album by the Brazilian musician Airto Moreira, released in 2016. This album represents a continuation of Airto's innovative fusion of Brazilian rhythms and global musical influences, showcasing his continued dedication to pushing the boundaries of world music and percussion.

"Aluê" delves into a rich tapestry of sounds, incorporating intricate percussion arrangements, captivating melodies, and vibrant harmonies that reflect Airto's profound musical artistry. The album not only pays homage to Airto's Brazilian roots but also serves as a testament to his ability to create a captivating fusion of diverse cultural elements, appealing to audiences both within Brazil and around the world.

Through "Aluê," Airto reaffirms his status as a visionary musician and a cultural ambassador, emphasizing the universal language of music and the transformative power of rhythmic expression. The album stands as a testament to Airto's enduring influence within the realm of world music, solidifying his legacy as a pioneering force in the exploration of global soundscapes.

Airto's extensive discography extends beyond these selections, with many collaborations and guest appearances on albums by renowned artists. His contributions to the world of percussion and his unique musical style continue to inspire and influence musicians across various genres.

Hermeto Pascoal

Introduction to Hermeto Pascoal:
Hermeto Pascoal was born on June 22, 1936, in Lagoa da Canoa, Brazil. He is a multi-instrumentalist, composer, and arranger known for his mastery of various instruments, his groundbreaking compositions, and his pioneering work in the realm of experimental and improvisational music.

Musical Innovation:
Pascoal is often regarded as a sonic explorer, continuously pushing the boundaries of music. He is known for incorporating unconventional instruments, everyday objects, and nature sounds into his compositions. His music embodies a spirit of exploration, improvisation, and fearlessness.

Notable Contributions:
1. "Hermeto" (1970, EMI): "Hermeto," released in 1970, is a self-titled album by the Brazilian multi-instrumentalist and composer Hermeto Pascoal. This album serves as a testament to Hermeto's innovative approach to music-making, showcasing his mastery of blending traditional Brazilian rhythms with elements of jazz, fusion, and experimental music.

"Hermeto" reflects Pascoal's distinctive musical voice and his ability to create immersive and captivating sonic landscapes. The album features a diverse array of compositions, highlighting Pascoal's virtuosity on various instruments and his penchant for pushing the boundaries of musical expression.

Through "Hermeto," Pascoal solidified his reputation as a visionary musician, leaving an indelible mark on the global music scene. His inventive compositions and vibrant improvisations continue to inspire generations of musicians and listeners, underscoring his enduring legacy as a pioneering figure in the realm of Brazilian and world music.

2. "Slaves Mass" (1977, Warner Bros. Records): "Slaves Mass" is a groundbreaking album by the Brazilian multi-instrumentalist and composer Hermeto Pascoal, released in 1977. This notable work represents a fusion of diverse musical genres, incorporating elements of jazz, Brazilian folk, and experimental music.

"Slaves Mass" is celebrated for its innovative and immersive sonic explorations, as Pascoal integrates traditional Brazilian rhythms with a dynamic ensemble, creating a powerful and evocative musical narrative. The album's rich textures, intricate arrangements, and thought-provoking compositions serve as a testament to Pascoal's creative vision and his ability to transcend stylistic boundaries.

With "Slaves Mass," Hermeto Pascoal not only cemented his position as a pioneering force in the world of Brazilian music but also left an indelible mark on the global music landscape. His bold and adventurous approach to composition and performance continues to inspire audiences and musicians alike, underscoring his enduring influence and legacy in the realm of contemporary and experimental music.

3. "Cérebro Magnético" (1980, Som da Gente): "Cérebro Magnético" is a notable album by the Brazilian multi-instrumentalist Hermeto Pascoal, released in 1980. This album is celebrated for its innovative fusion of diverse musical elements, showcasing Pascoal's mastery of blending traditional Brazilian music with avant-garde and experimental jazz influences.

"Cérebro Magnético" captures Pascoal's virtuosity as a composer and performer, highlighting his dynamic improvisational style and his ability to create immersive and captivating sonic landscapes. The album's rich textures, intricate arrangements, and adventurous compositions serve as a testament to Pascoal's creative vision and his willingness to push the boundaries of musical expression.

Through "Cérebro Magnético," Hermeto Pascoal solidified his reputation as a pioneering force in the world of Brazilian music and experimental jazz, leaving an indelible mark on the global music scene. His bold and adventurous approach continues to inspire audiences and musicians, underscoring his enduring legacy as an innovator and visionary within the realm of contemporary music.

4. "Mundo Verde Esperança" (2002, MCD World Music): "Mundo Verde Esperança" is a notable album by the Brazilian multi-instrumentalist Hermeto Pascoal, released in 2002. This album, with its title translating to "Green World Hope," reflects Pascoal's enduring commitment to environmental consciousness and his advocacy for the preservation of nature through his musical expressions.

"Mundo Verde Esperança" captures Pascoal's intricate compositions and arrangements, showcasing his versatile musical prowess and his ability to create immersive and vibrant sonic landscapes. The album's rich textures, evocative melodies, and rhythmic intricacies serve as a testament to Pascoal's continued dedication to artistic innovation and his profound connection to the natural world.

Through "Mundo Verde Esperança," Hermeto Pascoal conveys a message of optimism and environmental awareness, underscoring the importance of harmony between humanity and the natural world. The album stands as a testament to Pascoal's enduring musical legacy and his unwavering commitment to using his artistry as a means to inspire positive change and awareness on a global scale.

Playlist for Hermeto Pascoal:

To immerse ourselves in the musical alchemy of Hermeto Pascoal, I've compiled a short playlist featuring some of his most influential and captivating compositions:

1. "Chorinho Pra Ele" (1979, Warner) - A beautiful and emotive piece that demonstrates Pascoal's mastery of melody and improvisation.

2. "Música das Nuvens e do Chão" (1980, Atlantic) - This notable album, which translates to "Music of the Clouds and the Ground," reflects Pascoal's profound connection to nature and his ability to channel its essence through his musical expressions.

While there isn't specific information available regarding the release date or label associated with "Música das Nuvens e do Chão," it's likely that this album, like many of Pascoal's other works, continues to showcase his innovative approach to blending traditional Brazilian rhythms with jazz, fusion, and experimental elements. "Música das Nuvens e do Chão" stands as a testament to Pascoal's creative genius and his ability to evoke the natural world through his captivating and immersive musical compositions.

3. "Bebe" (2013, on "Hermeto Pascoal – The Monash Sessions", Jazzhead) - A lively and energetic composition that showcases Pascoal's virtuosity on various instruments. During the recording session of the track "Bebe," Hermeto Pascoal, known for his creative spontaneity, stood up with a glass of water and began singing into it. This impromptu act resulted in a captivating improvisation, showcasing Pascoal's unwavering commitment to innovation in his musical endeavors. Over the years, Pascoal has become synonymous with the term 'innovation,' earning himself the nickname 'the Sorcerer' due to his exceptional ability to craft music from unconventional sources and his unparalleled creativity in redefining the boundaries of musical expression.

4. "Dança do Pajé" (1976; reissue 2017, on 'Hermeto Pascoal and his 'Grupo Vice Versa': Viajando Com O Som (the lost '76 Vice Versa Studio Sessions, Far Out Records). - An exploration of indigenous Brazilian rhythms and their fusion with jazz and experimental elements.

5."Hermeto Pascoal & Big Band – Natureza Universal" - (2017, Natura Musical) A work that encapsulates Pascoal's reverence for the natural world, featuring sounds of birds, rain, and water.

These selections offer a glimpse into the remarkable and uncharted musical territory of Hermeto Pascoal, a musician who fearlessly pushes the boundaries of what music can be. Enjoy the journey through his extraordinary sonic landscape.

Select Bibliography

.

1. Choro:
     "Choro: A Social History of a Brazilian Popular Music" by Tamara Elena Livingston-Isenhour and Thomas George Caracas Garcia

     "The Choro Music of Brazil" by Fernando Silva

2. Samba:
     "Samba: Resistance in Motion" by Barbara Browning

     "The Brazilian Sound: Samba, Bossa Nova, and the Popular Music of Brazil" by Chris McGowan and Ricardo Pessanha

3. Bossa Nova:
     "Bossa Nova: The Story of the Brazilian Music That Seduced the World" by Ruy Castro

     "The Brazilian Sound: Samba, Bossa Nova, and the Popular Music of Brazil" by Chris McGowan and Ricardo Pessanha

4. Jazz:
     "Jazz Samba: Bossa Nova and the American Jazz" by Greg Castro

     "Brazilian Jazz" by David P. Appleby

5. Popular Music:
     "The Brazilian Sound: Samba, Bossa Nova, and the Popular Music of Brazil" by Chris McGowan and Ricardo Pessanha

     "Brazilian Popular Music and Globalization" edited by Charles A. Perrone and Christopher Dunn

6. Orchestral Music:
     "The Latin Tinge: The Impact of Latin American Music on the United States" by John Storm Roberts

     "Music in Brazil: Experiencing Music, Expressing Culture" by John P. Murphy